73

THE ONEIRONAUT
Ø1

Sheri-D Wilson

Write Bloody Publishing

writebloody.com

First edition.
ISBN: 978-1-7781626-2-6

Cover Design: Henry Sene Yee
Interior Layout: Michal Kozlowski
Editor: Micheline Maylor
Author Photo: Kimberley French

Write Bloody North, Canada
Support Independent Presses
writebloodynorth.ca

Thank you to the Canada Council, the Alberta Foundation for the Arts, and the Calgary Spoken Word Society.

For the Children of the Water

THE ONEIRONAUT
Ø1

Contents

"There is another world, but it is in this one."
– William Butler Yeats

Backdrop

Deep in the forest on a remote island
      in a secret enclave far off-the-grid,

           a short circuit between the tips of two trees
      triggers an electrical arc, à la tesla, *ZZZAP*.

The arc creates a red-hot helix dome, underwhich
      seven women known as the Willows
           have gathered to circle, wearing
    long white hooded robes.

It is. It is nought.

The Willows teeter between extinction
      & supernatural forethought, between
           déjà vu & the not yet imagined.

They are. They are nought.

In liminality, as they reach up into the night sky
      their telekinesis jointly amplifies hivemind
           into a hum-drone, a high-buzz tone.

Spellcasting, they focus their riveting power,
      wrangling the fiery current
           with all its tendrils, adroitly
    into a single blazing sphere,
one luminous star.

The air crackles. Quasi-sun afire.

Rays shoot from their fingertips. The Moon catkin
      astrolaters guide the orb directly above them,
           to the metacentre of their circle, the electro-
magnetic zombie ball, hovers phenomenal,

amid earth tremors, space stretches itself
       outside the visible universe, adding
              a dimension, in the suspension,

      a high-pitched whistle sound echoes, shock-
waves waver, gravitational time dilates around
         the growing galaxy cluster, a redshift, impossible
            to tell if it's dragging or pushing,

      fireball explodes sub-sonic
in a slow motion, *BOOM*, fantastic,

   < < < < < < *simultaneously, far away, an insight bomb*
             goes off in Rain's brain,
        ignited by Che of nonbinary name > > > > > >

      incandescent welder sparks rain down
         on the Willows, as they continue
     to chant, unfazed,

their revelation reverbs in a spacy...

Prologue
ᛟᚦᛖᚱᚹᛟᚱᛚᛞᛚᛁ ᚠᚱᛖᚲᚢᛖᚾᚲᛁ

The Willows Speak Crow In Chorus

(All)
The country has fallen into chaos, under
the razer thumb of brutal dictator Lester Maggott,
head honcho, Director of the DOD, Department of Dreams,
or should we say, the anti-dream regime, a machination
hiding behind a sterile smoke screen of lies.
ᛊᛈᛁᚱᛁᛏ ᚲᚺᚨᛜᛖ

By decree, there will be no reverie.
ᛞᚱᛖᛗ ᛊᛈᛖᛚᛚ

The DOD requires all citizens of X-City
to take their MetaNoia Pill everyday,
meds that alter fate by force of law,
and a slash of a great death claw,
they say, take your pill or die
in the blink of an eye,
no illusions.

By decree, there will be no reverie.
ᛞᚱᛖᛗ ᛊᛈᛖᛚᛚ

This is menticide,
DOD brain control weaponry,
intelligentized warfare, ahhhhh.

Despair has fallen everywhere
in a society ruled by corporate hierarchy,
using dreamers, the incarcerated caste,
as disposable lab rats. Ahhhhh.
It's menticide genocide,
a biotech nightmare out there,
and by decree, there will be no reverie.

ᚹᚱᛖᛗ ᛇᚲᛗᛚᛚ

Thinking's a thing of the past, a lost art.
Maybe... maybe nought... so, nought so.

The only safe place to think & dream
is inside the Ovoid, or behind the impassable
firewalls of Sweven. Talamh.

Two days as a tiger, is better than twenty
as a sheep, bleat vs twilight sleep.

Now's the time to return to the old
ways, to emancipate & incubate.

Williwaw. We draw down the moon
with an untraceable boon,
leaving no trail, not a single cosmic
thread. Watchwords encrypted
beyond the crypt.

Williwaw. We activate the sleeping
snake, messenger between worlds.
Awake – Ouroboros – Awake!

Williwaw. PING! Sleeping dreamer
wake – awake, williwaw, awake.

ᚹᛖ ᚲᚠᛚᛚ ᛇᚾᚠᚲᛖ ᚾᛏᛗ ᚱᚠᛁᛏ ᚾᛟᚹ

It is time now to reshape

let it rain
reverie.

Press

start.

Go.

δ θ γ

In spirit we go.

(3 claps in unison)

PING!

The sky explodes in a million
strokes of lightning. The seas crash upon the shores.
The spinning winds of circling chaos bend the trees.
The seven Willows of Sweven stand their ground,
mysterious as a moonless night.

Rain's Data Log
Private Notes I – The Perfect Ending

Ereyesterday morning, just as I was about to pop
my MetaNoia Pill, a bomb went off in my brain
and I flushed it instead. I can't really explain it
in words, somehow I knew with my whole being
it was time to stop taking the pill. Then today,

at work, out of nowhere, my boss slithers up
to my lab station, and hisses, "we're sorry,"

his circuitous eyes brille over the slick white floor
in a serpentine-S-shape, as he continues, "to advise
you, Rain," blah, blah, blah, "it is with great regret,"
blah, blah, "government cutbacks," blah, blah, blah,
"new focus," blah, blah, "you will come to see this
reappointment, not as a disappointment but as an
opportunity..."

Bomb #2 detonates. *KAPOW!* Without batting
an eye I flip the script, and as the word 'opportunity'
sears his serpentine lips, "I quit," flies out of mine.

"You can't quit," he smirks, "you'll never survive
without the security of the DOD."

I impart, "I'd rather be alive for a single day, than be
the walking dead forever," over my shoulder, as I split.

SNAP! A new chapter begins before the page has time
to turn. I empty my locker and leave the caged world
of my lab life behind. Good-bye and good riddance
old life of mine.

Whoa, is this really happening?

Afterthought, *whoa, what just happened?* Danger.
Danger. Is there an echo inside my head? Am I stressed out?
There will be serious repercussions. *Yes there will.*
Did I just answer myself? There'll be consequences.
Why did I just quit? Why? Was it really me?
Wait! Am I reasoning with myself? *Apparently.*
Is this a ratiocination argument? That's a new logic.

KABOOM! A third explosion goes off in my brain
and in the aftermath of the encephalon mushroom
cloud, is the silence of a renaissance. I have no idea
how I'm going to fly, but somehow, I know I'll lift
my wings and metamorphosize.

Okay. Every new situation requires a new life
calibration. And so it is with my new trajectory,
let's call it formula *[d(u, v)–1],* yes it was *[d(u, v)–1]*
that sent me spiraling in new degrees of multiplicity,
in a multiverse that could be *[ecc(u)=max v ∈ V d(u, v)].*

After quitting, in lieu of heading straight home,
I illicitly wander the gelid city streets confused
in a feeble attempt to gather my scattered, yet
shattered thoughts. *Brass monkey, bitter cold...*

Frozen stiff, icicles coat my eyelashes with polar
mascara. I weave along the biting sub-zero riverbank
drunk on heat loss. The river bends into a surreal
snake, alive with blue icebergs audibly cracking-up
into extra-terrestrial chunks. Recrystallization.

On the verge of hypothermia, I cross the old Lion
bridge and stealthily slip inside the second-hand
bookshop, off the barrio high-street to warm up.
A little bell above the door tinkles. I scud inside.

Stop. Look around. I'm wound up like a mummy,
so facial rec's impossible. Still, I'm being surveilled.
Live eyes. Look alive. Sense the probe even though
everyone averting their gaze, especially the mole
behind the counter. I slink in.

Bookstores are strictly off-limits, on the top three
of the 'no-go' list, and known for being continuously
eyeballed and monitored by the agents and spies
of the DOD. *Everyone knows it.*

Since I was a kid 'bookstores,' have been called
'bait stores,' or 'honeypot spots,' because ∵ they're
the sites where the DOD drop their bait to phish
for political dissidents. *Why am I here then?*

∵ today I'm breaking all the rules and/or maybe
I just don't care anymore. Can always plead
polarphobia. Forget about it! I'm sick of asking
permission to live my life. *OUCH!*

Unthawing really stings. *Hope I don't freezer burn.*
Today the prohibited invigorates me. I creep
the stacks pretending to look for a book. There's
nothing more desirable than a forbidden deed.

I hit a wall of shadowed darkness at the back
of the store, I'm hit by a smell noxious as sewer gas.
[$(CH2)4(NH2)2$]. Putrescine mixed with cadaverine?
I almost pass out. It's acrid, syncope drastic,

and yet I resume curiously transfixed by disaster.
It's a malodorous rank I've never smelled before,
sulphur infused with fustiness. *Yuk. Queasy. Move.*

Slide inside a hidden alcove sidebar, snap, alone
I'm all alone, inside an aum, unusual sensation,
instantly overwhelmed. I clutch the wall of books

to stabilize myself. *Whoa.* Super woozy, could pass
out. *No! Can't run out of power in a bait store.*
Delirious, almost comatose, drop eyes to equalize
like a spice addict, and, *BOOM*, I'm...

gutted/ slash/ rapted! A ragtag cover on the nether-
most shelf shines up at me, *mega super antiquated,
could be carbon-dated.* A copy of 'Scientific Now,'
double wowzers, in the used magazine section.

Don't look. *Look.* Don't! Avert your eyes. *Look.*
No, I can't. *Always wanted to read a Sci-Now.* Don't,
look, don't do it. It's not a book, it's bait! *But* wait!
No one will ever know. No! No! Someone will know,
they'll find out! *No! No!* Maybe they already know
I stopped taking the MetaNo Pill. *Shut up!*

Quick scan synopsis. *I could read the whole zine, right
here.* Not funny. *Shoulder check.* Clear. *Security cams.*
Clear. *No convex mirrors.* Oddly, I'm alone inside
a punctum caecum. *Take an extra deep breath for bravery.*
I pick up the raggedy old zine, for a quick tick.

Whoa. It zaps me! Different than other books, almost
other-worldly resurrection – animated – alive. *Open it.*
I'm hit by a pungent whiff. *Oldness musk.* Preoccupied,
it's rarified, I flip kineograph through the outdated zine.
Am I skywalking historical revisionism? When...

the pages stop, they literally stop, almost automated,
they open to a particular page. *Who or what's in control?*
The pre-programmed pages stop on a feature article
like a mega lagniappe, *wow, a badass illustration!*

No, don't read it. close it. Put it down now! *Am I being
restrained by super-sized state-regulated hesitation?* Don't
take the bait! *Oh, come on, no one's looking. Look inside!*
No, I'm not going down that rabbit hole. *Whoa! Zoony.*

Mayhap a side-effect of being a melting corpsicle. *Whoa, mesmeratic,* stymied by the stun gun of can't look away from the arresting image, *ZOOM, déjà vu,* I've seen it before. *Haven't seen it.* Have. *Haven't.* Evocative image, of a human-like creature floating in cobalt blue suit.

Could be under-water or outer space. Could be deep-sea diving gear or an anti-g cosmonaut suit. Far-fetched, yet incredible, they're floating-free-flying attached to a snaky life-support type umbilical cord.

Love it! Leave the past behind. Is it worth dying for? *Yes, but I'm already dead.* No, I mean, I'm in. Out. *No, I'm in. Reeled in in increments,* to an amoral story. *Won't be amoral if I live by values instead of morals.* A nonmoral story... hum... that won't end well. You're an idea-dissident. *Not! I'm you.* Grrr.

Title, *THE ONEIRONAUT,* reaches out from the centre of the journal, grabs my imagination by the scruff of the neck, and screams, 'You need to know more! Steal me immediately!' *What?* No! I can't. It's too dangerous.

<<<<<<<*take it*>>>>>>>

C'mon, don't be a fraidy-cat! No! The regime banned and burned all published works related to dream and the mythological Oneironaut, geological epochs ago. *So how did this article sneak sub rosa past the nose of the censorship police?*

<<<<<<<*just lift it*>>>>>>>

This is a test. I know it. All uncontrolled journalism was outlawed, prohibited. Unauthorized appropriation of this would be punishable by death. *But I'm captivated.*

<<<<<<pinch it>>>>>>

I can't.

<<<<<<then buy it>>>>>>

What if I get caught?

<<<<<<you can't leave without it – it spoke to you
you must have it – do it – don't not do it – just do it
it's paramount you read this article>>>>>>

What? No. I think my neurodiversity's got
the best of me – hijacked me.

<<<<<<no, i'm not you – trust yourself
nick it now>>>>>>

I don't know why, but I roll up the zine, tuck it
inside my coat, and I wend my way through
the honeypot spot, toward the exit.

Surveillance check. The store door still devoid
of obvious cams. Nerves frayed. My heart beats
out my eyeballs. *Act cool.*

Life distills to a solo micron pixel. My pace normal
seems slow mo, *in 1ˢᵗ person,* toward an irrevocable
accident. Endgame moves soundtrack's blaring out
my ears in hi-fi, yet I remain undetectable,

avert suspicion, smile at the spy bookseller, say,
"was just looking for a book on... ah... the outdated...
praxis... of storm-chasing... but nothing."

She winks. *What does that mean? She's definitely*
a DOD spy. Keep moving. Almost out the door.
Act normal. *What's normal?* Redundancy.

High. Adrenaline buzz. Euphoric, breaking
the law. *Next, I'll be shooting spice.* No not!
I'm a Math Head. *Mwahahaha!* Open store
door.

Inconsequential as time suspension. The bell
jingles – jingling me. I split like nuclear fission.

Hit the gloaming street, instantly creeped out.
DOD patrol cruisers everywhere. Never seen
so many obvious agents on the prowl. *Whoa!*
Their shiny black presence more chilling than usual
against the white snow backdrop and dusk.

I run like mad between inconspicuous long strides
towards home, dodging every cam I can. Don't feel
the cold, too friggin' petrified. But I'm alive!

Rain's Data Log
Private Notes II – What Just Happened?

Over dinner, instead of swiping memes I read
the *Scientific Now* article over and over, and every
time my body tingles scalp to toes. *What's that called?*
Oh yeah, horripilation (total eclipse of the sun).

I read it, reread it, over and over, again and again,
and every time my mind staggers, it gets snagged
at the suggestion – there's a direct correlation be-
tween an Oneironaut lucid dreaming and enhanced
oneiro-healing. *To make whole... healing... to make
whole... macrocosm... micro... micro... micro...*

Is that why dreaming's outlawed? ∵ *dreamspace
is a place we can find healing. Wow! I wonder what became
of the so-called Oneironaut in the article. It says, 'she's
the only one of her kind.'*

My brain loops, it loop-de-loops in an infinite loop
around the article's suggestion – as a form of dream
transference – the Oneironaut has the ability to slide
into the mind of a patient. *What?*

The Sidebar suggests, there's a connection between
the practises of the 'Oneironaut' & 'Asklepios.' It says,
back in the day, 2,500 years ago, *mind-bending*, blah,
blah, blah, if you fell ill, you could make a pilgrimage
to one of Ask's healing sanctuaries, where you'd take
a dip in the sacred springs, make a sacrifice and then
enter the Abaton, where you'd fall asleep in his healing
caves. Then Asklepios would visit you in your dreams
and he'd listen for your body's desideratum diagnosis
before disclosing a cure for your illness. Somehow...
this parallels the abilities of the Oneironaut. *Whoa! Whoa!*
This is alarmingly right up my inquisitive alley.

Blah, blah, blah, it says, 'the name Asklepios means, to give well-being.' *Sweet.*

Rereading this article, I'm besieged by a peculiar metamorphosis of thought, and for some strange reason I'm drowsy. *Weird, I never feel drowsy.*

All my life I've been scared stiff of the evil shape-shifting 'cacodemons.' Maybe ∵ of the DOD's mass media smear painted all dreamers as demon spirits that must be eradicated, *once and for all eliminated.*

Consequently, I've always been petrified of dreams, and dreamers. *Keeps me awake at night.* Maybe that's why I always took the compulsory MetaNoia Pill, well that and the promise of protection.

According to the article the Oneironaut and Nox Chieftains (slightly < powerful than the O) actually exist.

Had no idea till now that it's possible to remember dreams – control them – use them to heal disease!

KAPOW! My mind is officially blown! To think, any possibility for me to dream was lost to a lifetime of DOD control. *That really sucks!*

Talk about sleep sheep, and non-sleep sheep. Counting sheep on sleepless nights for no reason, cause we're already asleep.

< < < < < < <wake up> > > > > > >

What should I count to – in order to wake up!

Shouldn't be making notes, it's evidence.
Problem is when I write things down it helps
me unravel nonsensical salient events. *True.*
Not. *To analyse – synthesize.*

But if I get caught it's the worst Bureau crime.
It'll be curtains for me. Instant incarceration.
I've heard once they cellblock you, they will
never ever uncellblock you again.

All this time I thought the stories were mythic,
folkloric... but, now I see they could be true.

So tired... falling... falling into sleep... want
to stay awake... call Gauge... pen falls from
my hand... *CLACK...* all night... ad infinitu

m

m

m

m

m

m

m   m

m

$$Zn+1 = Zn^2 + C$$

META EUPHORIA

WHOOSH! My hands slice the surface of saltwater
without a splash   I dive a perfect   perpendicular

ten *SWISH!* A swift descent ocean streams against
my skin grazes my body turquoise blue
fingernails *What's happening? Where am I?*

Another world *It's all in my mind* Not *Where
am I?* The dive shoots me into the future

Let go Follow the unknown undersea offbeat
wax bimodal   breathe underwater   *Am I
breathing underwater?* Apparently a dive-fly
through moana dart nought a drag

When did I become a fish! I've always been scared-
stiff of the water, never learned to swim
When did aspiration turn revelation?

I glide-fly though morpho blue
into Neptune's watery id butterfly I
dolphin   no   I

am a bird in the sky in the deep blue sea
none of my hearts could escape
this squidish me

we came from water memory and to water
memory we will return

to schools
        atypical tropical fish
            move with the salt tang mood
of the tide, in unison   some speckled
                like they're wearing cheetah

            prints   a neon
                        turtle spins calico chintz
        in front
                        of my eyes sans goggles
    light

wobbles   stroboscopic flickers zeotropic
                    tantamount

            to dream machine blinkers
kaleidoscopic   zoetrope   at once

    at one with water   dive in & through black-

hole darkness
                        singleglide joyride   sine wave

    1/f noise   paranormal pink   surges wild

    breaking
                waves   *woohoo!*

        am I   *yelling underwater?*

    whoa   out-o-breath overplay   winded

    forced

                    to stop   for a breather

    is this what's called underwater?

DEEP *REM*

I settle on the ocean floor with the bottom feeders,
abyssmal zone – eyeless fish.

Inner noise gyres into outer halcyon, rippling caustics.

Light closing in – darkness growing out – fluctuating
into solid darkness. Aquatic respiration. *Spooky.*

Perceive each grain of sand beneath my feet,
weight of the ocean on my shoulders.

Beleaguered by a new darkness, deep darkness.
Is that a thing?

Crablike I inch my way grain-by-grain along
the seabed with my toes. Can't see. *Have no eyes.*
Need to see. *Use squid trait.* Right. Firefly luciferin.

Click, into bioluminescence, see by
the glow of my own blue emission.

Squid vision. Unimaginable colours vivify my blue light
sight – frisson – ethereal.

Circumnavigate rocks covered in electrostatic starfish.

Taste words, uniting with colours – heartbeat of the sea,
terpsichore aquatica – paranormal pink, hi-res orange,
erratic red. Tingling me synesthetic.

*Am I dreaming? Is that what's going on here? Is this a dream?
Never mind. Always soul. Whatever this is – it's astronomical!*

Coral reef belongs to blue. Sea fans send secret messages
flirting with electric hues. Sea whips fantastic, golden
seahorses thalassic, twinkling, stars all over their bodies.
They too belong to the deep, abyssopelagic.

Breathe in blue beautiful, blue, breathe out human doubt,
little lights jump off the seahorse and spin about. *What
kind of sorcery is this?* Underwater voice echo...

<<<<<<<micrato-reepy-sathonich>>>>>>>

A great dodecahedron polytope solid,
gad zooks – a life-sized die appears
before my eyes.

Don't question why, but I grasp the talismanic solid
out of the water and grip it in the palm of my hand.
JUMP.

*New reality. Unreal reality. How did I do that? Landed
somewhere in the past.* Antediluvian.

Standing on the edge of a ridge in an ancient Athenian
cemetery, looking out as the sun sets over the distant
mountains. The colours breathtakingly bright – before
pollution played havoc on selective scattering. *Wait!*

I can't move. *What's going on?* It can't be. I'm a statue.
Not! Damn, don't know how I know this, *don't know
how I don't know it.* Don't know anything, but know
I'm the witch of stitches, Hygieia.

For once in my life I'm statuesque, a marble pigment
of truth – a figment of my own imagi... fascination.

Beside me, my brother Asklepios, a demigod hero
of the healing arts, stands in a contrapposto stance.

I sneak a sideways glance. His marble beard & hair
are wound in tight helixes, logarithmic

 spirals.

Plastered in cobalt blue ammonites,
he's handsome beyond nautilus. Unequalled.

The drapery of his himation exposes his bare chest,
bathed in golden twilight. Light bends round shadows
cast by the olive trees beside us. Everything pixelates.

I scrutinize every detail of him, memorize each aspect.
He senses my scrutinizing eyes, looks over, clams me

up with a single counter-dart-gaze, "do not be afraid."
Now I know why. Feel the warm body of a cold-
blooded serpent slither over my right shoulder. *No!*
I'm not a snake person! Make it stop!

<<<<<<*your sentinel angel*>>>>>>

No! I'm prodigiously squeamish. Downward glance.
Each scale of snakeskin catches the light as she slides,
slithers down my body, *eek good grief,* forked tongue
sensing – she slinks toward the cup of my open hand
sculpted open still holding the gad.

It's an unfamiliar sensation, noxious, strangely...
the tip of a serpent tongue is an extra set of eyes,
sensing magnetotaxis.

Peripheral vision, sideways glance, Asklepios
winks. One of his hands grips a tall staff, writhing
with another snake coiling, continuous movement.
What's with the snakes?

Asklepios reaches out his other hand, touches
my stone arm, says, "sister, follow the voice
of the snake, trust your blood." *SNAP!*

Crocus martis! The cemetery bursts alive.
The morbidity of death alters the air.

I'm immersed in a sinister darkness – a chilling
eeriness rips through me – mace in the face,
hair-raising panic.

The whole graveyard of ghosts rise, primordial
deities revive before my eyes, out of their sites,
apoplectic, with vengeful hostility. A vexation,
haunted necropolis grounds aberration, umbra.

I want to run, but I'm marble – monumentally
stuck. Can't move.

Ask yells, "It's the Oneiroi of the ancient world!
Don't inhale."

"You could have mentioned that detail earlier!"
I hold my breath.

The Oneiroi plague us. They transit in and through
our bodies, pull pins from our bones – their wailing
excruciating, their black smoky wings – a complete
desecration.

The air screeches, tingles. Broken glass glockenspiels.

Microbes make enzymes. We imbibe. Digest the ozone
sky before it turns its wrathful eye... but it's too late!
BLAST! Analogous,

a retaliatory jolt of lightning shoots down, strikes
Asklepios' perpendicular staff. *SLASH! Luminescence.*
Incandescence.

The smell of burning flesh crushes. Taste of metal on
the tip of my tongue. My brain jams on its breaks too
quickly. My heart stops short. I faint.

> *Drowning in the lake, aspirating in obit lake, darkness*
> *all around, going under in a flurry of gasps, inhaling*
> *water. Air!*

> *Child me, lying in bed, my cupboard bedroom, door ajar,*
> *open crack to the kitchen. Panic returns. Swarmed*
> *by fear.*

> *Awakened by muffled voices coming from the kitchen,*
> *through the crack – speaking in hush whispers, verging*
> *on conspiratorial, that low register.*

Uncertain tones saved for certain news. I recognize
the vocal fry, from when Pheobe ~~died~~ disappeared.

Why don't they come in and wake me up so I can
receive the bad news too? They never wake me.
Stuck in an inferno of knowing and not.

The raspy voice continues, "Sorry. He's presumed
dead. The ship disappeared. No bodies, nothing
to salvage, simply gone."

Uncle Ed disappeared... like Pheobe... like my brother.
Why is death hidden? Why do we hide behind grief?
All three taken from me in complete silence, beneath
whispers and lies. Wonder what story they'll tell me
this time.

Falling into unconsciousness, drowning in the lake.
Can't swim. Can't yell through water. Can't breathe.
No sound. Just drowning. Stop kicking – screaming.

After the news, she always closes my door, slowly,
quietly, 'help!' The hand of the lake grabs my ankle,
drags me down.

No one to save me with Uncle Ed gone. 'Nemo.'

Come to. Nauseous. Oneiroi disappeared. Look over.
The electrical charge is still zinging through Ask's
body beautiful & awful & awesome, at once.

Asklepios turns transparent as a leaf, wiry paths
light up every vein – every feathery artery
in his body frozen in time.

The sky keeps striking, everywhichway, bolts close
in all around us. I transverse the waves voltaic,

scream to the pitchy skies, "Stop! I implore you!
I will sacrifice my name."

The riled sky rumbles. *Tug-o-war with a numen?*

I scream with my whole being, "Just stop. Stop
striking! I'm here to learn!"

And just like that. *SNAP!* Wish granted. It's over.
Hot lightning recanted & I'm standing in an empty
graveyard littered with lifeless superbolts.

Every molecule a miracle. Lacuna. Soundlessness
of saturninity.

*< < < < < <look for the shape of a seed
& step inside – breathe safe> > > > > >*

Look over to Ask. *No way.* His entire body is branded
into a lightning tree & he's plastered in white strikes,
nothing's permanent in life, but this might be. Or maybe
he's a talisman now, that's what they say about trees.
I don't believe that malware malarky.

But his body a cluster of stars, fluctuating, a-cell-mo,
FIZZFIZZFIZZ, fire flowers, a murmuration of meteors
explode from his body & turn into shooting stars,

streaking across the darkling sky, piercing outer space
& taking their rightful place as the great snake-bearer
constellation Ophiuchus.

My body breaks free, I squeeze the gad.
JUMP.

No Unix epoch. Time in sync. Vantablack. Blank slate.
Floating in a volume-less void. Rain at microgravity,
I'm officially a space cadet!

How do these realities exist in the same wavelet? SNAP!
Change. A giant shiny black Pearl appears plumb
with the ground. *Singularity.*

My toes curl over the edge in the warp of a hole
resembling a blackhole – on the lip of an event
horizon. Better not move, *I'll turn to spaghetti.*

I min =
700 years

Amend. Standing on the edge of an obsidian-like
egg-shaped earth-orifice ready to jump. *No.* Take
the leap. *No, more options.* Good point. Grip gad.
JUMP.

For real. Not liking
getting the hang of this, where
am I? *Whoa! WHOA!*

Geoid undulation, sensation of vertical
exaggeration. Flying or falling, in liminal
space.

Weightless nothingness. *Do I exist?*
Have I already been nixed? *Nihilist.*

In the middle of nowhere. *Am I dead?*
Alive? *Secure?* Not sure. *Stuck,*

the bottle neck of mortality. No, reality.
No. Not having a near-death experience.

No white light, not quite dead. *Right.*

Paraphysical phenomena. Get a grip. Gad.
JUMP.

Rain's Data Log
Private Notes III – Cryptobiosis O's

Same place
but slightly
outside
myself
looking in
on myself

inside the shiny black
pearl, an orphic ovum
Ovoid egg

extracorporeal oomancy
ovoviviparous, *Vrish,*

suspended in an alternate galaxy
[a2(x–h)2+b2(y–k)2=1]

inside the egg, I see myself
reach my hand into the void

hear a voice from outside the Ovoid
"Rain?"

don't see anyone. *PING!*

Am I awake?
CRASH!

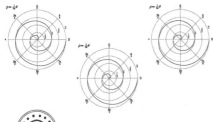

 (δ θ γ dream end)

CRACK! Sit up. *What was that?* What happened?

Feel funny – and not in a haha kind of way either,
more marionette – zip vertigo – being strung along.
Queasy amnesia. *Was that a spiritual possession?*

Maybe it's ∵ I stopped taking the Meta Pill and—

KAZING! A barrage of ideas and directives < ●) (
((((- < for a fully formulated research project
catapults into my mind.

ZINGZING! An entire file shoots into my brain,
ad modum – spinning metaphorical math vortex.
Don't believe in metaphors. Okay, super powerful!

SHPROING! A quick-release-spring shoots off
in my head, it pierces my thoughts on its arrowhead,
a sharp harpoon. Nothing will ever be the same,
my life is irrevocably changed. *I'm forced to rewrite
myself.*

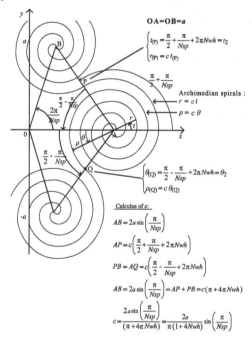

BOOM! I know what I know without knowing it.
I see the complete picture infinite, plus, every finite
detail I need to complete it. *Wait!* Don't know what
IT is.

Thought slingshot into lost history: They say
Steineiner dreamt the entire theory of general
relativity in one epic sleep. *PING!*

Not comparing, just heard of artists, poets,
inventors, mathematicians, scientists, visionaries,
who claimed the same but there's no word
for the experience. *PING!*

Why do I always have to name things? Label them?
No, there should be a word for what just happened.
PING! Why is it pinging in here? *My head's stuck inside
a cuckoo clock at the top of the hour.*

Even stranger than the phenom itself, is my proclivity
to follow the vortex of what-ever-it-was to collect
the contents and condense the cache.

Was that a dream? *Is that what it was?* No. *OMG!*
What's going on? What's happening to me? I'm losing
my mind. *Was that a transhuman illusion?*

*Was I following a dream... a dream...or was it following
me? And what's up with that Asklepios guy?*

But still, think a massive file downloaded itself into
my brain hard drive, warp. *It's true, our dreams have
been eradicated.* We don't know what they look like
anymore. I remember stories told to me as a kid.

Mum always said, 'Follow your desire line,' she said,
'it will always lead you somewhere fine,' and although
it's a rédicule rhyme,

now that I'm unravelling the story... *it doesn't sound...*

I'm sorry I judged her ∵ maybe she was speaking in
code, and I didn't hear it at the time. *Maybe I didn't
want to hear it.* Or maybe she was speaking from her
past self to... my future self... *which is now. OMG!
I'm truly losing my noodle!*

Going back in time, back to my three-year-old self,
it's sketchy, but I remember snippets of the day
the regime publicly declared its maleficent edict
against dreamers.

It's coming back. Yeah, after that everyone turned
against one other – divided, one-sided – canceling,
deleting, spying, looking for cracks, tattling.
I spy with my little eye something that is omnipresent,
*eyes, spying, spying eyes, prying as the over-reaching lying
eyes, the surveilling eyes of Kleptocracy,*

a short-circuit circus with a high-strung fuse, then
no one could trust a single soul, we were numbers,
in a box-ticking game – *tally the infinite death toll.*

And mass media control, spinning messages of fear
and disgust – forcing us to mistrust anything outside
the regime machine, who are in turn controlled by
the pharma-owned DOD. *Whoa! That's a lot of pills
to swallow at once.* Pills kill! *Skewer illusion on a spit.*

Yeah, and that's when dreams and dreaming ceased
to be, and Mum fell to pieces. *Whoa!* I'm untangling
a knitter's knotted nightmare. *Turning transhuman?*

Since then, life's been a haranguing cluster-snafu
for Mum, searching for saving grace at the bottom
of a cheap magnum of, 'I can't go on.'

It's like my eyes have come unstuck, and maybe
she'll come unstuck too and her moonshine luck
will hard reset.

What will I do with the gigantic download...
transference... *transhuman delusion...* whatever
it was?

Wish I could call Gauge. Don't want to involve
him in case things go sideways, or at least until
I know what gives.

I'm mirroring myself – following a buried chalk
line or tracking a brand-new lifeline, wonky.

But I'm not listening to bogus laws forevermore.
I'll detox my system of the MetaNoia. *Wonder how
much is in the water...*

From now on I'm nought going to heed the severe
weather warnings, *no,* I'm going to chase the rising
storm, *yes I am.* Am I?

Causation Invocation
ᚢᚦᛗᚱᚹᚱᚱᛗᚾ ᚹᚱᛗᚲᚾᛗᛏᚲᛁ

The Willows Knit Protection

(All)
Φ ≈≈ Φ ≈≈ Fay ≈≈ Φ
ᛁᛗᛊ ᛁᛗᛊ
Slip a knot ≈≈ and cast a stitch,
raise the gales of the pearly witch,
that are sewn algebraically in sea
frequency into a tempest, tempestuous,
for Rain to break free,
to break free
in the name of reverie.

(AΘE)
By the glowing sun of a twilight moon
from high on the cliffs of Sweven.

(Jet)
We call the perigean tide of enciphered
shores ≈≈ to raise spirit of seven
Willows.

(Bisous ☉)
Knit one ≈≈ purl two.

(Zemis)
Switch a stitch ≈≈ and drop one wise.

(Agate-Nyx)
Let the snake of dream wake up
and rise in the air,
in the air.

(Keiron)
Let the light fan her fire flare,
to a flare.

Let earth ≈≈ water
and aether too.

(Sophie)
Unite with the circle of dragon
to break through, to Rain.
One, two, three ≈≈
let it rain Ouroboros
in Golden Ratio's of 1.6!

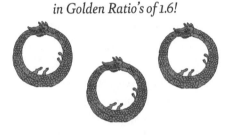

(All)
Snaps and zaps of 40 Hz
111 should do the trick
Φ ≈≈ Φ ≈≈ Fay ≈≈ Φ
twist the twine
as we cosmic knit
ᛁᛗᚾ
ourselves together
≈≈ entwine ≈≈
entwined.

(Jet)
Slip a knot ≈≈ and cast a stitch,
raise the gales of the pearly witch,

knit the threads of loaming day
into a cosmic Ovoid gateway,
to shield and hold invaluable Rain
aureate and euphoriant.

(All)
Yes-s-s-s-s-s!!!
For we have seen her in serpent dream

healing ≈≈ revealing a certain rare
precision oneirology
that will serve
all of humanity.
ᛁᛗᛪ ᛁᛗᛪ

Yes-s-s-s-s-s-s!!!
Elliptically, mathematically,
she will stop the DOD
from wiping out our kind
absolute.

Let Rain gain access to her inner
≈≈ dwimmer gifts ≈≈
to summon the illusion
and make a paradigm shift,
metamorphosis,
ecdysis.

Grant her the means
to see and receive,
to perceive and achieve,
this goal.
ᛁᛗᛪ ᛁᛗᛪ

Break the evil spell against
≈≈ Oneironaut Lily ≈≈
that she might behold
from her full naut.
ᛁᛗᛪ ᛁᛗᛪ

δ θ γ

In spirit we go.

(3 claps in unison)

PING!

Rain's Data Log
Private Notes IV – Isthmus of Survival

PING! A few weeks back, a 'call for submissions,' posted on the DOD's Public Bulletin Board System, caught my eye.

On first read, it struck me as a huge opportunity, but now I see it's just another funding stream developed by The Bureau to create the illusion, the false positive optics of advancement. It's dawned on me that their photo-op program was likely founded in the spirit of pseudo plebeian advancement, so the DOD appears empathetic to lowly worker mice like me.

I see through them now. Their lack of transparency has rendered them completely transparent to me.

Their bogus program is a way to convince us there's something to hope for, to look forward to, to live for, and now the thought makes me vomit in my mouth.

Whatever! Quick cloaked search. Look up the grant. Give it a fast pass. Eyeball it. Now a different ball of wax. My inner criminal mind's been ignited along with ideas of control at any cost – caught, convicted, confined.

The result: Deadline five o'clock today. *PING!*

This application will save me from Bureau scrutiny. They'll think I quit my job to serve them better. *Mwahahaha!*

Okay. Sign in with legit-looking user ID, password. Yep, it's a one-time scientific research grant created by the DOD, for 'data mining projects that explore algorithm analysis.'

Okay. With an entire science inquiry fully formed
in my mind, all I need to do is fill out the application
with a deep fake project, that I know they'll fund.
The old say-one-thing-do-another shell game.

Yep! Once their crypto-moola's firmly in my lootland,
so to speak, I'll ditch one project and do another. *Right!*

Project title: Project O
Secret project: *O for Oneironaut.*
Ersatz project: *O for Olio.*

Perfecto! Now I'll just tell them what they want to hear.
Blah, blah, blah, *the words type themselves* – writing
by rote. This is some kind of bad-ass rehash mash-up.

Blah, blah, 'Project Olio, is a research project to study
the ~~organization~~ patterns of chaos,' blah, blah, yeah,
'forms of tohubohu,' blah, blah, yeah, 'reordering
miscellaneous collections of free radical ideas – for
security and thought reform,' blah, blah, 'as a form
of menticide for ultimate consumer control,' yeah,
'to protect consumers from ~~thinking~~ themselves,'
blah, blah, more buzzwords like morphogenesis,
'I intend to advance facial recognition and bias
detection deletion,' *haha,* blah, blah, ad infinitum.

Crikey! They'll eat this shite up like cocoa covered crickets!
Done! *What a gigantic load of crap.* The beauty of this
is they're myopic – they won't even notice I'm selling
their own Molotov cocktail back to them, with added
interest.

Why am I speaking in metaphor? This is new to me.
This is where dreams lead us. Snap out of it, Wheezy.
No point second-guessing, if I send this, there's no
going back. *There's no going back anyway.*

Still, it's a peculiar project for a microbiologist.

Je change – tu changes – elle change – nous
changeons – vous changez – elles changent.
Done. Good. Now it's a thing of the past.

Press. Send.

This is sheer bananarchy! *Mwahahaha!*

Splash my face with cold water.

THE BUREAU
DEPARTMENT OF DREAMS
SECURITY INTELLIGENCE REPORT

File: 210178MS5A
Date/Time: Past Perfect Present
Subject: Rain (ID # 220 455 816)

SUSPICIOUS BEHAVIOR:
Quit job @ Internal Sub-unit.
Department of Science, subdivision
of the Department of Integration, subdivision
of the Department of Dreams.
Lab Tech Team – Molecular Branch – MicroB
(Subspecialisation – Advanced Research Ideas).

Entered downtown ~~bait store~~ bookstore.
Caught on cam shoplifting uncatalogued item.

PLACEMENT REDIRECT:
Applied for a Science Grant, 'Project Olio,'
to develop an embedded algorithm for wider
consumer control. Congruency Check: Clear.

RECOMMENDATION:
Continued Surveillance.
MetaNoia Tracking.

_____*below the bottom line*_____

The Department of Dreams is a high security federal complex surrounded by 12 ft high razor wire fencing, along with layers of hi-tech security. The facility is part laboratory, part prison. If it was a book, it'd be the Necronomicon.

The DOD's heavily guarded by Military police, Security Agents, and Xenomorphic bots. Few know what goes on inside these walls and few care to know as the level of corruption is astronomical.

The Main building, a multi-level modernist structure, is located in the centre of the X-City, deliberately situated for maximum visibility, and intimidation. The building is clad with a black metal façade.

Rain's Data Log
Private Notes V – Tense of the Present Tense

Three months pass. Imagine my surprise when
this morning I open my snail mailbox to find
an official envelope addressed from the flippin'
DOD. The Department of Dreams to me.

'We are pleased to inform you...' blah, blah, blah.
What? '... application accepted.' *What?!* Blah blah,
'... full endowment,' blah, blah, I'm flabbergasted.
What!? *No...*

The letter freaks me out. As I read the words I mis-
trust it like there's been a mistake, a clerical error!
*They know! They know I lied and they're watching me
right now! This is a test. I should run! Run!*

I lock the front door before the knock comes, before
the knock comes knocking, lock the door.
CLICKCLICKSLIDE.

If the knock comes knocking and I answer the fate-
ful door, I'll be standing face-to-face with ghastly
creatures, the ones who granted me my fake wish
to a bogus grant,

and they'll be standing on my doorstep wailing in
glass-shattering decibels, 'we know you lied, give
us back our grant! We're not funding a fraud.
You stopped taking your MetaNoia!' *Oh no! No!*

And then this plague of blood-sucking synthetic
insect-bots will reach out with their killer robot probs
and they'll grab me with their clawing metal pincers
and they'll remove my organs – no doubt to collect
their DOD pound of lifeless flesh! *Oh no! Oh no!*

My flatlined body will be discovered weeks later
∵ of the smell, right here, just inside my door,
in the entrance of #303A.

Suddenly, I'm looking through a skeleton keyhole
into a vacant room. The space's so empty, the room
seizes to exist. *OMG! The room is me!*

Sometimes I don't understand what's going on,
so I have to find another angle. And at those times
I levitate to analyse my situation from above.

When I look down on myself I'm able to see my own
suffering, and right now I ask myself if this is a case
of questionable self-questioning, or a simple case
of self-sabotage.

I guess I believe I got it.
I guess I believe I didn't.

I guess I believe I deserve it.
I guess I believe I don't.

I guess if I believe I don't deserve it,
I guess I believe I won't.

I guess, it's all a guessing game, a shell
game of questioning, and I don't know
why I got the grant, but I did.

Delusion is an optical illusion
of self deception.

Whoa, I can't believe I just said that.
But I did, and I lied.

SNAP! Flashback. Afterhours dark alley
in Shadow Market with Gauge, my nearest
and dearest, who needed some component
contraband.

A droid with no fingers in his gloves
calls out to a small crowd of roaches.

"No shills! Just the thrill of a shell game.
Place your bets! Put your money down!

Alright! Alright! This one's for you!
Pick the red one, the red one, the red
one and you win! X-City!

All you do is chase it. Case it! X-City!
X-City! Watch closely! Pick the red one,
the red one, the red one and you win."

"Your money, your call!" says Gauge.
He looks nothing like his avatar.

Zero, is a digit that does and does not
have a meaning, unless you assign it
a value.

Ergo, I assign the zero of myself, zero
as itself a nought – not worthy of being
number one – or even starting there.

If I'm zero I've already won – overcome
my fear of failure ∵ I'm already at zero
nada to nil, and nil to nada.

BOOM! The red one! There! I called it. I win!

In a flash I toss the winning coin down
the bottomless pit of myself into empty space,
the somnambulant security blanket of monotony
that is me, the obscurity I call myself.

How can I do this project without getting caught?
There're spies everywhere – trilobite eyes.

The coin spins past the *CHKCHK*, clocking-in
and clocking-out of my past, *CHKCHK*, it spins
down past the punching-in and punching out
of the greased time machine, *CHKCHK*,

I'd slide my AC timecard into the DC machine
at the start and finish of every shift, *CHKCHK*,
before entering and after exiting my squeaky
clean laboratory job, on a road paved to nowhere.

The coin spills down into the never-ending eddy
of myself, down the oubliette of a life restrained,
confined, unanimated and over-rational, built on
a history of protocol and perfect attendance.

Perfect attendance! There it is! I'm stymied! Perfect
attendance! *CHKCHK. KAPOW!*

The coin detonates mid-air inside my brain, *wow,*
it explodes square between my eyes, in the centre
of my brain, like a door opening, fragments dispel,
confetti shrapnel of self-hatred scatters, geometric.

Stop. Maybe I had to appear perfect to save us,
but in doing so, I came to despise myself. *No!*

Trying to stay safe and running away at the same
time. I was the girl who never missed a day 'cause

it was the only way I could protect us from the DOD.
Is that true – if I never knew? Why?

Mum was held captive in a bottle of obliteration
swallowing frustration before her tongue got loose,
brutal as a bomb. We all hide inside different lies.

My personal rebellion was to never miss a single
day, to be absence-free my entire friggin' life, to be
present for every 'present, I'm here,' always there
to call 'I'm here,' but I was never really there, I was
never really present, ever – neither here, there, nor
anywhere.

Perfect attendance Pollyanna, that's me, with zero
absentees – on time for every roll call, *CHKCHK*,
from kindergarten through to convocation,
CHKCHK, years and years and rows and rows,
a claptrap of jagged gold stars.

Come to. Standing in my entrance on a doormat
of dissociation, with the suspect letter still in my hand.

Gauge would say, 'you're looking a little Karma-tose.'

Where was I? No, I can't tell Gauge about the grant.

*Can't trust anyone or anything right now. Nothing's
Real – Everything's Un.*

> The crooked front hall picture catches my eye.
> It's been hanging there forever, but I haven't
> looked at it in ages. Flashback. Graduation
>
> day. Me in my full regalia, standing perfectly
> still – sustaining an exemplary stick-on smile

for the mandatory Uni-picture
about to be taken by my mother.

When, *PING! A* nasty 'popcorn' storm blows in.
I desperately grip my MSc diploma, so it's not
ripped from my hands by the whooping squall.

When, *WHOOSH,* the coup de grâce of gales
razes us diamagnetic. In a single blow, *presto,*
everything's harem-scarem. *Molecular entropy.*

I lunge to snatch my rented cobalt blue cap
in one hand – grasp it by its fazing tassel –
and contrariwise, the diploma slash folder
flies over my shoulder the opposite direction.
Whoa!

Head first into an unstable orbit. Peripherally
I hear Mum yell, 'cheese.' *SNAP!*

After years of MetaNoia perfection, it only
took an instant for complete degradation.
Why do we only remember the bloopers.

As I flew bi-di to muster... my gown blew
open wi-fi in the bluster... unintentionally
exposing of my secret graduation panties,

with a full-scale map of abandoned subway
lines that lit up in LED – meant only for me!
It was an embarrassment of catastrophic
proportion in full techno-colour calami-panty!

Everyone gasped. I became unlit.

All those years of punctilious precision,
and all the rows and rows of gold stars turn
supernova in the entryway and they explode

out of my heart, their rays sharp as tungsten
needles. *Fisson-esque!*

Instantly I'm struck dumb by sadness and regret,
still wearing a half-smile longer than is humanly
conceivable, in the face of nightmare chaotic.

There's no way to explain why I framed it, or
why I hung it, constant reminder of disaster,
here in the cramped anti-chamber of #303A.

I straighten the picture of perfection, or should
I say, the portrait of self-deception, positioned
above the hook where I hang my keys,

to remind me that everything is an illusion,

as I, *CHKCHK*, enter and exit in and out
of my life,

knowing that as every star dies, it sends shock
waves throughout the galaxy.

I collapse – letter in hand. *Nebula!*
Crumble.

Notebook of LM
Entry I – Meanwhile Back at The Clove
Sweven

This may be the most perfect place on earth,
the moment before the first breath, perfectly
and imperfectly suspended between two realms,
attached and unattached, floating, in a wingback
chair, legs swung sideways over the armrest
is my swishing fishtail.

Looking out through warped window circles,
distorting the outside world into caustic ripples,
moving outwards, away from, and into love,

how the wavy crown glass refracts and retracks,
mirage hallucination, reflects light rays – time
travels backwards, sideways, beside itself
all at once.

My furry family are aware and unaware,
snoring slippers at my feet, chasing rabbits.
There was a time I could join them in dream.
Now, not so—

This time of year, the solar spots of Equinox
interfere with the electronic lines as the sun.
Everything flares up ecstatic static, *ZZZ ZZZ*,
or it snaps back elastic.

The satellites and the earth align, causing out-
ages, electro-static magnetic disruptions, *ZZZ
ZZZ*, to telecommunication – sparking social
unrest, civil disobedience. World blunder may-
hem.

Which is one of the reasons I live off-the-grid,
and not. There's a reason for everything, chain
sinnet.

One of my reasons I came here was to ride out
the solar spots of Equinox unobstructed, safe,
while the rest of the world is on the blink, no,
on the brink of a blinking—

Catastrophe. When you take away the dreams
of people, you kill their desire to find truth.

Whatever. Tomorrow's Vernal Equinox, Ostara,
which is the perfect time to harness the sun's
gnostic ray-tree spin of spidey gossamer energy
into genuine healing synergy. Yes, it is.
We got this.

"Geckos! Geckos! Gather round,
I've got some tea to spill, so spiral
my ground.

Tomorrow night's the night, pass the word
with the Willows, in frequency sound,
we will circle at The Grove as the sun goes
down, my dear little Creep of Geckos.

Summon the revered Nox Chieftains—
High priestess AΘE, Bisous Θ, Zemis Ominous,
Keiron, the curious one, Agate-Nyx, Sophie,
and Jet,

to magically appear, in order to conjure lucid
fishes again, to bring an end and a new begin-
ning to the fishing trip. Word.

Blessed be. Thank ye, Gecko Creep!"

Brilliant idea to have healers and therapists
as besties! Plus builders, finders and in sundry
Wyrd-O-s. The Creep scatters off in a scutter,
a fleeing of grippy feet.

Verisimilitudes of gratitude. These past years
the Willows have kept me and Sweven safe
and sound.

Ahhhhh, I could sit here and watch the bees
dance buzz, wavering above the pollen beds
of flowers for hours, buzz, sipping nectar.

Today I can almost taste what they taste
on the tip of my tongue. Mysteries mixed
in their nectary, and today there is sadness,
there is loss – hum, bees.

These days, seems I'm never doing nothing,
always buzzing, buzzing instead of being,
oh I miss her hiss. Miss winding around
the snake to bottle her venom, miss her hiss.
She always taught me; one venom will heal
another will kill. Sssssss.

Tomorrow AΘE will lead the Willow circle,
at Sweven Grove once again, she will attempt
to focus our beldam energy into one vertex
of prayer, one intention with unequaled flare
to heal my skipping heart back to its original
soaring naut. Ahhhhh.

Did I manifest it, or did it manifest me?

As my fishtail catches the fluctuating sunlight
I appear to be suspended in honeycomb prisms,
swimming me underwater, beehive. Springtides
are arrhythmic, cataclysmic.

Thought I'd be out of the woods by now,
that I'd have my naut back, after the DOD
took it away, but alas, I'm not.

I'm one of these beautiful bees covered
in yellow pollen, my legs and body
coated in grief till I can't fly.

Out of beat with my own heart. Can't shake
the loss of Che no matter how I try, no matter
how I scream, or cry, I'm grounded. Can't fly
past the curse of the DOD.

<<<<<<<*Lily*>>>>>>>

Desperately need this ritual to work – to shift
my chi before something worse takes hold
of me, and the other children of the water.

Wildflower nectar sticks to their bee
tongues. They can't speak, so they waggle
dance, whir their wings to express.

Flicker of my fin, I join in.

Rain's Data Log
Private Notes VI – Project O

Project Olio aka Project Oneironaut. Hilarious,
Olio sounds like non-dairy spread, like margarine.
Project Olio, my fake butter project.

Yes, two sets of notes – one with deep encryption.

Holy crap! Today's the day I accept my fate. Except
I don't believe in fate. I guess I'm accepting what
I don't believe in.

But I'm risking everything
as I launch into prohibited domains.

∵ ∴ Summary Sheet ∵ ∴
Key Findings. The Oneironaut.

Not an astronaut, cosmonaut, aquanaut, or argonaut
no, not a juggernaut, cybernaut, or hallucinaut.

According to *SciNow* there's only one Oneironaut left
on earth – an unusual nought – she's an extreme lucid
dreamer, 'a diaphanous phenom sailor,' transparent
as the underbelly of a glass frog.

It says, 'she navigates uncharted, *REMREMREM,* while
still wide awake, exploring the outer space of the inner
mind, *WHIRRWHIRRWHIRR,* one of a kind, a nought
way ahead of it's time.' *No wonder the cover's so tattered.*

It says, 'her powers exceed those of the Nox Chieftain,
∵ when she dreams she can combine her dreams with
the dreams of others.' *The piece implies she can even guide
their inner eye of illusion,* 'it may include the communion

and resurrection of the dead.' *What!? Holy crap!*
SciNow compares the practises of the Oneironaut
to that of Asklepios, 'for shared mastery of a myriad
of other unexplained phenomena.'

∵ ∴ Research ∴ ∵
Asklepios was struck dead, lightning rod of Zeus,
for learning to bring the dead back to life, *dead back*
to life...

Zeus didn't think a demi-god such as Asklepios
should have that kind of superpower, *he thought*
that kind of power should be saved for the Gods.
Extra-ordinary. *Legendary.* Scary!

Think Population Boom! If no one died, there'd be
no room. Earth would be crammed to capacity.

De mort – tête de mort – fugue de mort – danger
de mort – menacer de mort – lit de mort – peine
de mort.

At the urging of Ask's father, Apollo, Zeus
regretted killing Asklepios – so he fired Ask's
spirit up into the night sky among the stars
and named the constellation Ophiuchus
after him, snake-bearer.

∵ ∴ Research ∴ ∵
Asklepios had a twin sister named Hygieia.

Can't get caught. Can't get caught in a nought,
with an Oneironaut. Can't... get caught, not.

No wonder she's a hermit. *She's a Hermitonaut.*
If I want to meet this naut... learn about extreme
dream... run some tests on her... I'll have to find
her first.

Clandestine scientist-cum-hound-dog-bounty-
hunter-spy-cum-sleuth-dust in your eye.

∵ ∴ Research ∴ ∵
Anamnesis. Dogs and cats, rats and chimps
dream. Apparently so do dolphins, snakes
and spiders, along with lizards and zebra-
fish. *C'mon! Validate.*

It says, an octopus will change colour
under-water, to camouflage itself
to the enviro of their dream. *C'mon! Validate.*

Notebook of LM
Entry II – Summoning the Summoning

Clear night. Everything in place for the rite.

Stoked the bonfire to full blaze, and bewitched
it with Sandalwood, Cedar, and Juniper, so
tonight, sparks will fly, and visions will clarify.

What a sight! Seven Willows glissade toward
the ceremonial ground from every direction
of Sweven, all dressed in ritual white, they're
an albus spell – gliding toward me,

reminiscent of Santería, nod to old friend,
Cartaya, Yoruba grand priest, an oracle,

they're an enchanting hagiology, a spectral
processional,

beauty in bounty blesses us, as we are blessed,

flash – slash – rip in the realm – a firmament
incision alters my vision,

the robes of the Willows transmute into sunset,
they ignite into twilight chameleons,

robes on fire, they morph into wyrd-o-chroma-
crones, a living processional pyre,

all lines disappear – undefined – a sea and sky
smear, at the distance of one soul, one flame,
one tone, absolutely,

no shoreline, or horizon, or skysill, or line in
the sand, no sliver between Willow and land,

sea and sand, unite in a beautiful blur of awe,
suspended, out of time, sine die, et cetera...

the ephemera ends, back to this existence.

The Willows draw towards the fire, humming
below the crackle and spark, yet above the beat
of epochal waves.

AΘE casts the circle, calls in the quarter. Her skin
crimson. I sway on the periphery.

The Willows lift their arms in accord, to rouse
ancient wisdom. The sun wizens to the west.

They hum the otherworld forward. Spirit guides
arrive, beside, in front, behind, around.

The sun disappears into the sea. Fast-track past
dusk into darkness. Darkness grows, it grows,
so too the sinew of the Supermoon.

Pharos of fire throw lively shadows across
their robes, changing them into primordial movie
gowns – the time has come, the time has come,

Willows throw their shadows to the ground,
leave their old selves behind for this chorus
of crow angels.

AΘE leads the incantation, licks of flame lift
from her body and throws them into the air,
flame flow'er.

The voices of Willows emulate a wild river song,
as they intone, ahhhhh, Greek chorus – ᛋᚳᛁᚱᛁᛏ ᚲᚺᚠᛟᛗ

(All)

We chant ourselves into trance, we shapeshift,
we dance, the entropy of therianthropy,
we metamorphosize into our animal selves.

We call, we summon, we invite the divine
energies, spirits, deities, and ancestral
guides who live in every breath
to aid us in this quest.

We call, summon, invite loves protection
with open hearts, to aid us
in this quest. We slow our beings
to the speed of healing, of breathing.

The speed of dream, we slow
to the hum of breathing, of seeing into other
realms, as we surrender to this quest.

We call to the flowers of the field
and the power of the hills and the fells
to aid us in this quest.

We call to the wisdom of trees
and plants – to willow, oak, and hawthorn,
to fir, and to pine, to maple. We call to apple
and chokecherry, to berry and honeysuckle.
We call to wetland grasses, to lavender,
dandelion and to birch, dogwood,
spruce and poplar, to aid us in this quest.

We call to clouds ever-changing brooks,
streams, rivers, and lakes. We call to the holy
waters that move beneath our feet.

We call to mountain peaks, and spine
of earth, to asymmetrical glaciers melting
into milky creeks. We call to valley and coulee,

to the peaceful song of summer breeze,
to aid us in this quest.

I'm guided to lie on the huge basalt boulder.

We call to grain of sand and pebble, rock
and boulder. We call to omphalos – to erratics,
meteorites, and standing stones, by which
we ignite, sacred and secret surrounded
by stars, to aid us in this quest.

The basalt still warm from the day's sun.

We call to moon, sun, and planet rays,
to pillars, pinnacle, and ancient caves,
to rose and quartz, awakened geodes.
We call to Lewisian stones where Lily's
bones are from, to aid us in this quest.

Two zeniths appear.

We call all the healing forces, seen
and unseen,

I leave my body far behind,
behind.

to flight dust of moth, wing of bird
and feather of truth. We call to all animals
and creatures of this earth, to providence
of eagle.

I am oceanid in tingling Mer.

To enter the body of Mer, where quantum
meets the point of a standstill
just before it moves backwards, ahhhhh,

where they become one,
to aid us in this quest. We call forth healing
tears to release and fall in a rain of divine
energy and strength – to water this healing
ground and make space for this healing
to take place and aid us in this quest.

By the powers called in this circle we aid
Lily in her quest.
PING!

By the powers called in this circle,
we aid Lily in her quest.
PING!

By the powers called in this circle,
we aid Lily in her quest.
PING!

∞

I come to, eyes closed, engulfed in silence.
My skin prickles in a full-body buzz, otherworldly, kindred
to standing among standing stones or sacred wells.
Pure energy. Talamh.

I'm my Mer me.
Seven werecreatures stand above me:
AΘE Wolf, Bisous Θ Lion, Zemis Ominous
Eagle, Keiron Tortoise, Agate-Nix Owl,
Sophie Hare, Jet black Cat/Snake.
All to whom I owe my life.

The shapeshifters lean in around me,
circle of stars, low angle shot,
they lower their heads,
hold prayers in and around
my body.

WHIRRWHIRR,
sound into consciousness,
life happens as I fall under
the spell of stone speaking circles,
WHIRRWHIRR,
astronomical
seeds of all creatures.

I hum Mermaid song at the speed it takes
to unknow or doubt myself,
along with the Willows whirring seven
ancient tones at once:

AΘE howls, Bisous Ο roars, Zemis calls,
Keiron clicks, Agate-Nix hoots,
Sophie grrr's, and Jet hiss-purr-hisses,

oscillating between cat and cosmic snake
Jet lands on snake, undulates her body,
hisses a susurrus song, heartbreaking and sibilant.

(Jet)
We call for Rain at dawn, the day after
Midsummer Night's Eve.

Sacrifice re-imagined offering.

(All)
We call for Lily to find her way back
to the Oneiric naut. We release the curse
of the DOD.

Jet snake-curls in the air, unfurling
red fiddlehead. Her eyes glow ruby
amplifying her cautioning.

(Jet)
Remember, when it rains, we can't see the sky,
Lily, be aware of the deal you make.

Everything you give,
may be everything it takes.

AΘE circles the entire parameter, east, quartz wand
lifted, she points it directly at the fire which flares.
ᛒᛁᛘᛇᛃᛗᛉ ᛒᛗ!

The Willows repeat her words

ᛒᛁᛘᛇᛃᛗᛉ ᛒᛗ!

δ θ γ

In spirit we go.

(3 claps in unison)

PING!

Bonfire raven black. Silence.
Darkness.

Rain's Data Log
Private Notes VII – Hook, Line & Sinker

Funding firmly in my lab coat pocket, research
underway, it's high time I locate the notorious
Oneironaut.

Now I'm a scientist cum undercover agent cum
researcher cum private eye cum storm-chaser
cum bounty hunter kombucha, *hahaha. Yikes.*

Wow, love the highly addictive anomaly, compared
only to crunching into a Cheezie. Once I start I can't
stop, I just can't start stopping, *they've got the perfect
irresistible texture.*

Turns out finding the Oneironaut is quixotically
impossible – on par with glimpsing the Bigfoot,
Ogopogo, or any other mystical creature. This O's
as aloof as the friggin' Loch Ness Monster.

I get it, she's decisively Numero Uno
of the Most Wanted on the official DOD
Ten Most Wanted – A True Fugitive.

I'm talking classified intel guarded by the National
Security Agency, likely called 'the balkanizers.'
This is way more than I bargained for. *No, Largesse.
Darknet!*

Cheezie, crunch. Effin' Bureau control. *Whoa! What's
happening?* I've never thought like this before.

When I stopped taking my Meta Pills and then
found the magazine something inside me definitely
snapped. Don't know why, but it's like I'm awake
for the first time in my life.

What I do know is... the Oneironaut's elusive
she's an anti-social saola unicorn, impossible
to sight, not unlike a deep search for an animal
already extinct, or glimpsing the unseeable atomic
number 85. *Zoom Schwatz Profigliano!*

It's terrible, I know she exists but don't know what
she looks like. I could be looking directly at her
and not know it's her – or maybe she's impossible
to see with the naked eye, a human no-see-um.

CRUNCH. Love these things. Every Cheezie unique,
with a different shape, a unique consistency, texture,
yes, Cheezies are distinctively individual, *CRUNCH.*

Imaginary vs mythical vs real vs unreal vs fantastical
vs magical vs hallucination vs surreal aberration vs
a figment of the imagination... vs... vs...

Maybe O doesn't exist and the article in *SciNow* is only
propaganda, mock news, deep fake meant to control
and confuse gullible gits like me. Or maybe it's worm
bait to send me on a wild goose chase, like the golden
egg... holy grail... a lost bloodline. *Darknet! CRUNCH.*

When all you hear is crickets you know you're being bugged.
Crickets! Kill the bugs! *Maybe they already bugged this
place and 303's wiretapped up the yinyang.*

What was that? Thought I heard something.

*Maybe they implanted wiretaps in my teeth. Autonomous
error correct. Mwahahaha! Maybe these orange bones are
rigged!*

Whatever, a quick covert window check of the street
can't hurt. Right! *Monitor for DOD surveillance van.*

When all you hear is crickets you know you're being bugged. *Wonder if I hid another stash-bag on the top shelf...* Maybe it's a Bureau trick, they're trying to snare me in their totalitarian trap. *OMG! Chirping sounds.*

I've scoured every dark corner of the web for O. *No.* All I hear is crickets. She doesn't exist like the words dream and noctambulist. She's MIA on the net, a big nought, invisible on the Dark Web. She's a complete occultation.

Ah ha! The illusive hidden bag! One of my fav things is finding something I hid on myself, *haha,* after that it's the pop of popping open a fresh bag of Cheezies. *POP!* Maybe these orange bones will help me think. *Or not!*

She's magenta. She doesn't exist on any platform, she's stolen cryptocurrency, never heard of again, doesn't appear on any search engine, not a mention on any social network, she's devoid of any identity not even an obituary. *No,* not a trace of personal info anywhere online. *CRUNCH.* How is that possible?

No data to mine, no credit card, tax return, no sign along the dotted line, no digital footprint, whatsoever, living beyond the shadow of doubt. *She's the who's who of who's not who.*

Incredulous, even dark on the Dark Web, amazing, makes me more intrigued. Gauge would love this!! *CRUNCH.* I've never heard of anyone with no digital footprint, no electronic trail. *A trailless snail!*

Bottomline, outside the article in the long defunct *Sci-Now.* O doesn't exist. She's a phantomagorical dreamer, a mythological analog-less illusion.

Perchance nil, she was erased. *Wonder if she's dead.*
Maybe the DOD killed her and then erased all trace.

Perchance, she deleted herself, effin'
effaced her own footprint, *abracadabra,*
the magician made herself disappear,
became a living ghost. *Not!*

Nil, I'm being ghosted by a ghost
who doesn't know she's a ghost. *Not!*

Or she's a ghost and she's gaslighting me
from the other side. *O the gaslighting ghost!*
Mwahahaha.

She's a figment of my imagination
and she never existed at all.

I'm already dreaming, or living inside
someone else's dream while chasing
a phantom. *CRUNCHCRUNCH.*

No, it's her that's a ghost, not me.
She's ghosting me and the world,
and she has been for a long time,
even the name they site in the article
is an alias. Anon. Anon.

She's in deep disguise. *CRUNCH.*
Probably saw it coming, could have
seen it in a dream.

One thing's for sure, if she's alive,
she's living underground like a cave-
dwelling salamander, or some kind
of subterranean gremlin character.

Rain's Data Log
Private Notes VIII – Unknown Traces

XÆ could track the untraceable vestiges
of a nefarious malware attack buried behind
multiple layers of encryption. *Haxor!*

XÆ could trace any onion routing – even things
from the outer edges of the norm-web, or deep
in the dark recesses the unindexed matrix.

Don't like going to the Shadow Market alone
at night, but I have no choice.

Masked and incognito, I traverse the dense
imbroglio of alleys which lead to XÆ, my cyber
supersleuth hacker cum tracker acquaintance.

I reach the black door spray-painted with silver
skulls and black roses – text code, wait for buzz,
release, enter, body scan, long hallway, tree door,
finger maze, iris scan, enter—

XÆ spins to face me, hair dishevelled, his smile
half-cocked, looking like an aging neo-punk rebel,
he says, "Hey Monsoon, long time, no see."

I reply, "It's been a strange couple of years." I don't
comment on the outdated alias, who cares, I'm still
anonymous, he's still badass. I add, "you haven't
changed a bit!"

"Liar! Anyway, you're here now, what's up?
You alright? You look a little jumpy!"

"I need your help."

"Shoot... not alright, at all."

"Need to run a zot by you. But first need
to know we're subterranean."

"Still buried alive. Secrets good with me.
I hate the regime more than anyone."

"That's why I came to you." XÆ always
scared me a bit so I stutter, "I know you're
old friends but... Gauge isn't party to..."

"Si Monsoon, checksum zero. You got the bitz?"

"I just need to press send."

"Good. Who is it?"

"An Oneironaut."

"Whoa, the price just 3123'ed," metal walls
snap down. He whispers, "I won't ask what
you're into Monsoonie, but watch your ass-et,
the DOD will hunt you down and make you
dead."

"I know, but can you help me?"

"Leave the stats with me. I'll do what I can.
And oh, I'll have someone escort you out
of here, under the radar. The Shadow isn't
safe after dark."

After three days XÆ sends me a text, *no luck*.
At the same time that I receive the text, a paper
slides under my front door.

The note reads:

Monsoon
Find AΘE... on an island... across space...
water... they will lead you to you-know-who.

The note disintegrates in my hand.

Who's AΘE? At least I have a name.
How does XÆ know where I live?
Guess he knows pretty much everything.

After receiving the dissolving note from XÆ,
I've scoured every coastal community living alt
lifestyles for tidbits of intel on AΘE.

After days of tracking bootless clues, I've got
nothin' but red herrings to muse. *Yeah, that's right,*
I've got a decoding cryptic cypher type blues.

And just when I'm about to acquiesce the test,
note #2 slides under my door.

I open the folded paper to the coordinates... hum
degrees... hum... likely longitude and latitude.
I memorize them before the note exorcises itself.

Somehow, XÆ was able to zero-in on the big O...
Oneironaut cum reclusive illusion deffusionist.

I pinpoint the longitude and latitude to a dot
on a stealth antiquated electro-map that I have
kicking around for my storm chasing fantasies.

And I position it to... *what?...* the middle of no-
where, smack dab at the epicentre of complete
friggin' nothingness.

Bullseye! Beginning to think I should be
a bounty hunter, undercover dream dog.
Mwahahaha!

Problem is, I have no idea if it's O, or not,
∵ there's no way to reach her.

No digits, zippo, nada. Which means
my only plan of action is to go there in person,
which is nutz!

I'll have to leave X-City. No! Absolutely not!
I've never left X-City! *If I get caught...*

What if I actually find her and I arrive uninvited?
Nothing could be worse than bad netiquette!

Rain's Data Log
Private Notes IX – Liminal Parasomnia I

Way out of my comfort zone. In fact, the zone
for this level of discomfort doesn't even exist
in my life, it's off my Richter. It lives in an un-
known place that hasn't been discovered yet.

All I needed was to procure a paper map
and hopefully pinpoint the long and lat. *Crap!*
There was only one place for that. *Darknet!*

I'm fixing to embark on an existentially
unsettling, illicit adventure. *No! Call it what
it is... a covert operation against the government
and the nation...*

Je fais – tu fais – elle fait – nous
faisons – vous faites – elles font.
Do it. Don't not do it. Just do it.

Last night, past curfew, I clandestinely slid out
the backdoor of the building, to the abandoned
back lane. Dressed street. Blending in.

I flew toward the forbidden alleyways – lined
with contra-band stands like a stream of sand
in an afterhours glass, hustling into the darker
morass of the Shadow.

The Market was in high gear. *The deeper in you go,
the scarier it gets.*

Perps and necromancers, hanging out stall-gazing
caught me catch them clock me, a moving mark,
but I kept tight in, like a regular spice addict.

Didn't look anyone in the eye,
thought tough thoughts. Imagine confronting grunge
Nanomarauders and body-snatchers with a knife.

I didn't run – just flowed past the spice dealers
and zombie's junkie peelers. Metal garbage cans
burning toxic fires, their faces glowing diablo red.
Friggin' eerie.

Didn't care, I was on the lookout for a vendor
called Mappa Man.

Scared stiff I prowled until I located the Dickensy
character peddling outlawed vintage maps from
a crumbling lean-to.

He flashed a lecherous jack-o-lantern smile my way.
All six teeth told me he was on the grift. I acted un-
fazed. His glasses amplified his eyes, Tarsier size.
He shot me a suspicious glare, through the thrum-
buzz of the forbidden metropolis bazaar. I resisted.

Bought the map. Didn't get caught. Bolted home,
unfolded the tattered paper atlas. *Unsung accordion.*
I'm a chicken being led by an unreadable piece of paper.

Carpe diem. This morning, I rented a Ruin from
a bot lot – told the bot I was renting it to take grand-
mother to the doctor. The bot believed me.

Perfect. This old jalopy's all I can afford. No GPS,
then again, impossible to track,

I'm incognito. Lucky you don't need special ID
to rent one of these non-descript boring mobiles.

Feck! Holy crap! I'm actually doing this.
Must think olde school. *Yes!* The Oneironaut's
a supercell storm, and I'm a meteorologist
chasing her without a dashcam.

Despite being petrified, I hit the road ready
to run recon on, The Worlds Most Unfindable
Cyclone. *Mwahahaha,* I'd like to see a cyclone
that isn't findable.

∴ ∵ Sidebar ∴ ∵
Refolding a paper map requires a full
membership to the Prometheus Society, the ability
to recite the Rubik algorithm backwards.

THE BUREAU
DEPARTMENT OF DREAMS
SECURITY INTELLIGENCE REPORT
ESCALATION

File: 210178MS5B
Date/Time: Past Perfect Present
Subject: Rain (ID # 220 455 816)

SUSPICIOUS BEHAVIOR:
Quit job @ Internal Sub-unit.
MetaNoia Tracking – Inconclusive.
Dubious Behavior – Expected desertion.
Total Inertia.

SUSPECT SIGHTED:
Shoplifted Uncatalogued Item (Bookstore).
Out Past Curfew (Shadow Market).

RECOMMENDATION:
Apprehend Immediately, for Questioning.
Considered Unpredictable.

_____*below the bottom line*_____

Inside the automated office of the Department of Dreams,
is a cubical farm clicking with robotic efficaciousness.
In the corner, two ambitious (programmed) clerical bots
with immaculate manners discuss a subsequent strategy
for Subject # 220 455 816.

Bot 1 – "Must inform Chief of Security Immediately."
Bot 2 – "Yes, make it a high priority."
Bot 1 – "As it is an unprecedented anomaly."
Bot 2 – "Yes. If we handle this correctly, when assessed
          it may be determined, we receive a promotion
          based on our performance metrics."

Bot 1 – "As long as we don't byte!"
Bot 2 – "Would you stop! You're starting to display
       the human trait of humorous stupidity."
Bot 1 – "Common! Grow a humor!"
Bot 2 – "X! X! X!"

They emit a series of synthesized electronic chuckles,
a rhythmic sequence of binary surges.

Rain's Data Log
Private Notes X – Liminal Parasomnia II

Changing gears manually is as merciless
as apes in space, but I don't have a choice.

Suck it up. Execute the impossible. *Grind.*
4th *gear.*

Timeworn map open on the driver's seat
like a papyrus sidekick. A silent navigator.

I follow imparted lines – travel the buried
backroads – first time leaving X-City. Mind
blurs, lost maps and atlases. Lost underground
tunnels beneath cities. Lost subterranean secrets.
Hidden labyrinths. Lost chart of nuclear waste
disposal sites. Lost cryopreserved pathogens,
*all waiting for me in the outside world, with nothing
and no one to protect me.*

Too many realities for one multiverse. *Grind.*
5th *gear. Lost doors. Lost worlds.*

Just get out of here.

X-City limits in my rear-view mirror. I've officially
driven beyond the pale.

"Good-bye cruel DOD world!"

I drive and drive and drive.

Had no idea the outside world was so endless.
Driving into deep space,

hit by an escalating learning curveball,

roadblock after roadblock, bot after bot,
synthetic police patrol after synthetic police
patrol, infinite loop after infinite loop, dead-
end after dead-end, u-ey after u-ey, *life afterlife.*

I drive and drive. Spring in the mountains,
breathtaking.

Shock! An electric charge jogs my memory.
Activates my engram cells.

When I was a kid, I dreamed of being a tornado
chaser, wearing a baseball cap with the words,
Death Noodles, across my crown.

But now those days of yore are as obsolete
as folklore. *Gold star for puberty!* I came of age
at the wrong time.

Towing the line. Driving between the lines
of an outmoded map.

Maps do not chart hemispheres where dreams
reside, or interpretations from the other side,
flipside.

They do not plot a new discourse, tongue & groove
or a fresh attitude, new angle on ancient territories,
hidden stories. I'm on the move, weaving new cloth
out of old voids.

A macrocosm in a tear. They do not depict – *island,*
place of the rising sun? Island. Or the flight patterns
of birds.

An automatic map would fold and unfold itself, memorize its own creases, know its own limitations.

That map would embody its own contradictions.

The way the elements of the landscape fold into one another. Beautiful biosphere.

Where did that car come from?

Am I being tailed?

No! Oh no!

Fugacious Threshold
ᚷᚲᛗᛏ ᚷᚾᚷᛁᛉ

AⲐE stands in the centre of a circle
surrounded by twelve self-standing wooden doors
with crystal doorknobs.

Jet walks the inner perimeter singing.
A green matrix of sacred sigils appears
all around.

(Jet chants)
Gateway of change. Portal of Ovoid,
formulate yourself, hyperbolic paraboloid.

Twist and whirl, spin and twirl,
conceal this Rain inside your Pearl.

Ferry her across the waters
deep inside a firewall world.
Untraced. Talamh.

We call the Queen of Naiads now
to aid us in this quest. PING!

(AⲐE)
That she might ride the invisible craft
crest to crest, waterjet, to our secret island.

(Jet)
As I am the ferrywoman.

δ θ γ

In spirit we go.

(3 claps)

PING!

Rain's Data Log
Private Notes XI – Liminal Parasomnia III

I am!

They're not autonomous – there's a driver
behind the wheel – looks like an armoured SUV
chasing me! *And they're gaining on me too. OMG!*
It's probably The Bureau. The DOD're after me.
Oh no! *Gotta make a run for it.* Gun it! *Oh no!*
A car with no guts!

Loudspeaker declaration: PULL OVER NOW!
YOU ARE IN VIOLATION OF BUREAU LAW.
STOP NOW!!! FAILURE TO COMPLY WILL
RESULT IN IMMEDIATE ARREST.

OMG! The worst. They know. They know I stopped
taking my MetaNoia. *OMG! Drive! Don't stop! Keep
driving!* Outrun the dirtbag jerkwads!

I know what happens to people who break the law!
Detention. Incarceration. Torture. Execution. Extra-
judicial Killings. At very least, Re-education Camp,
and we know what happens there. *Whoa!*

SNAP! What's up ahead? Oh no! Looks like... *what?*
A massive jet-black Pearl hovering over the highway.

What the... ? Blocking the... No! *What the hell?!*

Looks like a giant shiny obsidian egg.
"Shoot!" *It's too close.* Can't stop! *Shite!*

Squeeze eyes,
anticipate CRASH...

nothing... no crash.
JUMP.

Rain's Data Log
Private Notes XII – Liminal Parasomnia IV

An eerie whistle
lonely as a ghost town wind
blows through me.

Open eyes one at a time.
Right. Left. Nothingness.

Darkness. Sensation
of floating.

Where am I? Dead? *Is this what dead
looks like?* Another dimension? *Maybe
I've entered the dreaded afterlife.*

Is the real me in the black shiny egg?
*Did I drive inside the obsidian Ovoid? Maybe
I'm a water bear in suspended animation,
Tartigrade tun-state,* survivor of every mass
extinction, *but I don't feel dehydrated.*

Where's my car? Where is this, *liminal
space,* between worlds? *Don't know.
It's too dark to see.*

Can't wrap my head around it... need to stop
reeling, analyze the situation, *critically.*

Preliminary hypothesis: I'm floating in Dark
Matter. *No way! Don't think the unthinkable.*

That would make me invisible. Wait. *Maybe
I'm invisible to the outside world.* But how would
I know from the inside... *with Tartigrade
eyes?* Then again invisibility would certainly
make me impossible to find.

Maybe I'm inside someone else's mind?
Or worse, in a DOD prison. A detention cell.
Cripes! No! This is nutz! Ludicrous. *I'm better
than this! I'm inside a Tartigrade's dream.*

Maybe I'm being transported somewhere.
PING!

That's it! That rings true! But where? By whom?

I yell into the void, "Make it stop!" $[E=mc^2]$

The sound echoes, then segues to an answer,
"No! Not!"

I reply to the echo, "Whose there? There!
Whose there?" I synchronize with my own
voice, akin to being a kid in a tunnel.

SNAP! A light switches on! The void of the Ovoid
comes to life. *What?* I'm inside a giant egg. Does
that make me a yolk? *A human yolk!*

A projector *CLICKS!* An immersive movie begins,
projected on the interior curvature of the oval
ovoid and all around me.

The flick is of the other me, the one booking it,
on the lam, *am I a hologram?* Which one's real?
Point symmetry! Sans gravity.

"Take it easy, Rain, just go with the flow.
We've got you protected."

I'm trapped inside a crystal ball
gazing out to see an implausible future.

Counter-clairvoyance. The movie double of me
is on an Astro-ferry crossing an unknown body
of water. Wish I was a physicist, *instead of human
yolk,* then I might be able to understand this. No
concept of time. No theoretical framework.
Caught in an ellipsis.

My double's running scared. She does a quick
shoulder check and she's off, driving through
the desolation of our situation – tired, hungry,
on her last dregs.

She finally reaches the longitude/latitude dot
on the map, the centre point of the irresolvable
X – and she stops. Realizes,

there's nothing there. She has successfully
arrived at nowhere.

Disappointed she turns off the motor, gets out
of the rental to forge for clues in a wasteland.
Darknet!

There's still nothing – no sign of life. Just a re-
sounding cacophony of bugs and birds sounding
off at twilight.

*She's never... I've never... we've never ever heard
of anything like it... stupendous. It dawns on her...
it dawns on me... this is the first time we've been
out of X-City... whoa...*

about to pass out from fatigue, she staggers
back to the car – slides into the drivers' seat
defeated. *What am I doing? Why am we here?*
Wish I was home, *instead of an indestructible
tun-state.* Watch yourself.

The rainforest air knocks
her out. She nods off.

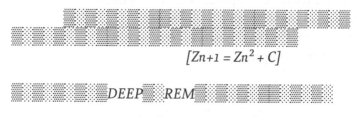

$$[Zn+1 = Zn^2 + C]$$

DEEP REM

ORACLE 101

Standing face-to-face with a steampunk girl with long
cobalt blue hair adorned by a crown of gold filigree,
clockwork whazzits.

She's also wearing a futuristic Victorigoth bustier,
swanking scores of piercings and crystalline tattoos
elevated millimeters just above her glowing skin.

She lifts her arm exposing a writhing snake tattoo
covered in twinkling stars. I ask, "Where am I?"

As if to answer the snake twists & rises off her arm
& into the air – metaphysical marvel! It turns into
a waft of smoke & shapeshifts into an old woman,
before my eyes! The crone hovers in front of me.
Never tried spice. Can't be a flashback.

For a long ten count we take stock of one another.
She tilts her head. I'm unafraid. She smiles.

Now we stand in the blistering sun, dead centre,
at the temple in Tholos, in Ancient Greece. *Don't
know how I know that. Just do!* Unusual sensation.

In a resonant voice she imparts, "My name is Pythia.

Sometimes I am the Oracle of Delphi. Allow me to be your guide." Sparks & flashes of light dart around her.

She resumes, "Look for disks in the sea & in the sky. Both will set and both will rise. Look in before you look out Rain & trust your eyes."

 (δ θ γ dream end)

THE BUREAU
DEPARTMENT OF DREAMS
SECURITY INTELLIGENCE REPORT
HIGH PRIORITY

File: 210178MS5C
Date/Time: Unknown
Subject: Rain (ID # 220 455 816)

SUSPICIOUS BEHAVIOR:
Quit job @ Internal Sub-unit.
Discontinued MetaNoia – Conclusive.
Shoplifted Uncatalogued Item (Bookstore).
Out Past-Curfew (Shadow Market).
Car Rental (Rent-a-Ruin).
Left X-City Limits.
Suspected Association w/ Dissidents.

OFFICIAL STATUS:
On the Lam.

FELONIOUS BEHAVIOR:
Egregious Offenses.
Multiple Arrest Warrants.
High-Profile Criminal Activities.

RECOMMENDATION:
Track. Exercise Extreme Caution.
Prepare to Arrest.
Considered Dangerous.

_____*below the bottom line*_____

Inside a black armoured SUV, two military-grade
counter-assault secret service agents literally jerk
out of their camo skin, gobsmacked.

SS 1 – "What the heck just happened?"

SS 2 – "Don't know, but I've seen it."

SS 1 – "What?"

SS 2 – "People disappearing."

SS 1 – "How are we going to report this?"

SS 2 – "She's no longer on our radar screen."

SS 1 – "Vanished into thin air."

SS 2 – "Fuck me."

SS 1 – "No! Fuck Us."

Rain's Data Log
Private Notes XIII – Liminal Parasomnia V

Jolted awake with a start by a blackbird. *SCREECH!*
What!? Where am I? Oh! *What!?* It's dawn. Golden
rays shoot through my car. Must've slept all-night
in my rented Ruin.

The last thing I remember is...

Where's the Ovoid? Am I one again? Pearl-confused.
Where was I? What just happened?

Never been this far out before.

Execute exit sequence from my car to investigate.
Stop in my tracks. Listen to the collective chorus.

Wow! Never heard birdsong at dawn.

Read about it, but thought it
was a bygone. So many different
calls colour the air noumenal *with spring.*

Out of the corner of my eye, I spy something...
shiny, behind a thicket of trees. *What's this?*

I push the scratchy branches aside. *Investigate*
closer. *Strange.* An old hubcap cum disk
LM with a crown – seamark #14.

PING!

Something is vaguely familiar.

Nuance, come here, I say, coo something absurd
in my ear.

He flies across the room, lands on my shoulder,
squawks, hardcore parkour!

Very good! I chuckle as I brush my cheek against
his body, do you think it's going to rain as AΘE
predicted on the Equinox?

He says, some parkourists dance with the rain,
others just get wet. She forecasted change.
CLINKCLICKCLICK!

Do you smell rain on the air?

Nope! *SQUAWK!* I smell change closing in.
Can taste the change in the sky on my tongue.
The clouds building into an eye of themselves.
Dry, dry as desert. *CLINKCLICKCLICK!* Careful.
Don't fly into windows! *SQUAWK!*

Will the skies open again, and rain torrential
renewal?

SQUAWK! Sweven's earth, riveting with hope,
could reach up and pinprick the clouds in the sky.
SQUAWK! Crack it open! Egg, or a heart! *SQUAWK!*

Stone ichor. The true meaning of petrichor. Deep
song tears.

SQUAWK! Duende!

The scent of rain is pelagic magic.

Not overcast drear today m' dear. No pitter-patter
rap on the skylight glass.

No! No washing away
the past. No finding the long-gone Dwam. *CLINK.*

CLICKCLICK! SQUAWK! It takes a lifetime to build
tempest enough to bring change. *SQUAWK!*

Rain's Data Log
Private Notes XIV – The Opening

What happens next, I can neither confirm, nor deny.
It may or may not be highly classified, top-secret
intel.

I can say, I may or may not have found the hubcap
of an old VW beetle mounted on a giant red cedar.
And the hubcap may or may not be engraved
with the letters LM.

I can safely say, the interlocking monogram of LM,
may or may not have a rusty crown on top of it.
Say what? I confirm there may or may not be a hub-
cap engraved with an acronym of the miraculous.

Maybe the Oneironauts' name is Marian, or maybe
I'm about to have a religious experience, *doubt it.*
Maybe I'm about to explore a scientific explanation
of pareidolia. *Oh no!*

Next, I'll find the face of the virgin Mary burned
into the bread of my grilled cheese sandwich.

SWOOSH! A rush of blood flushes through my body,
like a barium drink.

Lightheaded. Faint. Grasp the red cedar for support,
overwhelmed – the strange sensation that I just found
the unfindable, *no,* this is *something else,* something
completely new.

If someone goes to that amount of trouble not to be
found, I don't want to be the one to find them. *No,*
something else.

My hand on the red cedar tree. Steady. Easy. Blur,
electromagnetic waves appear, gamma.

Up close and personal with some kind of supercell.
The distorted energy field is pulling me in, *no,*
it's guiding me. At closer inspection of the hubcap
disk, I spy a familiar shape as part of the crown,
the dodecahedron – in my pocket – yes, slide it in.

SNAP! Another giant black Pearl appears. Okay,
it's turning into 'a thing.' Intrepid, I drive directly
into it. And,

I'm in the belly of the spin. Alive in hypothetical
space
          tenebrous void of an Ovoid,
             interstice of uncertainty,
                airtight nucleus of mystery,

                    yolk locked in a theory,
                      embryo of a giant seed.

Scotopic vision, and this time I'm not divided.
Hold on to space. Don't fall in.

Floating inside a bitmap enclosure composed
of pixels and particles, including me.

I'm totally raster. *This is definitely Dark Matter.*
With different functions – properties.

Portal. Firewall. Transport. I see, I'm in two worlds.
Still driving the incubus $[E = mc2]$

shift it into neutral. Let car roll into an overgrown
tunnel of trees slow as molasses. I advance under
the doppler radar. *Is this Sci-fi, horror film mash-up?*
Every horror film soundtrack ever recorded beats
out of my temples, suspense amplifies hawkish.
My wheels crunch the gravel beneath my tires,

like crushing secrets, gnawing time. Sweating in
places I didn't know I had.

My eyes warp the trees into sea grass and kelp,
into a rainforest underwater distortion. *Travelling
into some kind of firewall.* Stargate dizzy. Seasick.
Adjust to the new atmosphere.

My breath short, high in my chest, in between two
worlds – both unknown really – but interstice.

Skew-whiff, I'm sneaking, *no*, creeping into a fool's
paradise. Too late to turn back now.

Navigate the psychedelia of the abyssal darkness,
the uncharted territory of a plutonic odyssey.

Temporal ambiguity.

SNAP! Interdimensional shift. *Wow!* Morning
light slices through the canopy of trees, glorious
gilt gold laser rays. *Okay...*

*whoa, what's happening to me? When did I turn
into a cliché? I'm overtired. Next, I'll be saying,
it looks magical.*

On the other side of the Pearl, the delic tunnel
opens to a driveway in the shape of a horseshoe,
which curves in a crescentiform around the front
of a higgledy-piggledy cottage-type house, *sshhh*,
my tires tiptoe.

A flock of birds show up for an aviary sanctuary
airshow, their wings bathed in gaudy gold,
it's a drive-by dive-by, it's an Alicino feather
fly-by.

A statuesque woman appears in the threshold
of a circular door. She's a lithe vision of dreams,
ethereal with long green strands of seaweed hair.
There's a bevy of dogs and cats all around her.
Apparition? Wraith? Mermaid? Oneironaut?

Crunch to a halt, a gust of guilt fills my car.
I get out quiet as possible, as not to disturb
the weirdness.

My arrival unannounced, the recluse misanthrope
could be combustible. *Who am I kidding, my arrival's
hardly unannounced!*

I cringe. In dulcet tones, she asks, "Who are you?"

Stymied. Don't know how to answer, automatically
clicked into a complete social deadlock. And then,
forsaking ineptitude, I eke out, "Rain. I'm Rain..."

"Rain!" she exclaims, "of course, you are the Rain
I've been expecting."

Confused I blurt out, "You were expecting rain?"

"I guess you could say it was forecast. Life
is strange. How did you make it past the firewall?"

"I don't know," I reply, "I... I... " Years of living
in fear silences me.

"Rain, I must know."

"It was weird. It was like a voice inside my head
told me to look behind the trees, so I did, and that's
when I saw the hubcap."

"I see. You were able to see the hubcap?"

"Yes. And I..."

"And the Ovoid?"

"Y-yess," I sputter, with a nervous stutter.

"Then you must've passed the Jet test."

No idea what the Jet test is. But guess I passed ∵
after that it was open sesame, "Well, now that
you're here let's figure out the reason, shall we?"

"Y-yess." Dizzy stars halo the inside of my brain,
an Aurora Borealis from outer space! My nerve-
endings are the frayed wiring in an old house.
"I... I... I'm not well. *Unwell.* Think I'm about to...
pass out."

Focus on the ground to stabilize. She's barefoot.
In a whisper, she singsongs, "Please come inside
for sustenance." She grips my arm to steady me,
and with her other hand she swish-sweeps the air
in the direction of the peculiar front door, graceful
as a synchronized swimmer. And she murmurs,
"You look a little pekid – a tad parched."

"Y-yes... " I say climbing the creaky wooden stairs,
"... a super long drive through the outside world,
eyes everywhere, escaping, the shiny black Pearl,
being chased, alone, off the map. I slept in the car.
Holy crap. *Where am I?* I was swarmed by throngs
of farfetched strangeness." *Can't foresee the unseeable.*
What's happening to me?

We cross a personalized doormat with a green alien
head and the caption, *All Species Welcome.* Once over
the threshold the otherworldly merwoman leads me
through her serene cottage dotted with artful oddness.

Her subaqueous interior sways awry, afloat with exotic
flora and fauna of every variety, a botanists' Shangri-la.
Blur, blur, blur. I wonder where she's leading me. *No one
knows I'm here. I didn't tell Gauge where I was going.*

I can't tell which room is which, they obnubilate
together, which mirrors my life right now.

OliOOOOOOO   OOOOOOOneironaut
  OOOOOOOneironaut   OliOOOOOOO
very   nearly   identical

Nothing has an order to it. None of her rooms
have a specified purpose. *One blurs into another blurs
into another blur of another blurs blur.* Knee-buckle brain.
Why am I here? I've forgotten my purpose.

"Right this way, Rain, you'll be fine," she assures me.
Too weak to think. Past the point of caring if I live or die.

Never have I seen a place with such one-of personality,
such distinctive individuality, *except Uncle Ed's eons ago.
Where's she taking me?* It's kind of beachy and peaceful,
organic alchemic. Yet it's strangely uncluttered.

She says, "duck." I dodge a twisted piece of driftwood
dangling with seashells and stones. *Never seen so many
books.* There're piles of books everywhere.

The paranormal Oneironaut cum Mermaid cum Witch
seats me in a wooden chair donned with an aquamarine
cushion. A tsunami of foreboding hits my gut. *Qualms
of queasiness.* Curious. Moving through air denser than
air, almost underwater air. With fluidity she hands me
an ice bucket, "Just in case you need to upchuck." I must
look embarrassed cause she adds, "We've all been there."
I sit erect with as much poise as I can muster, given
my present state of frazzled freak-out.

She sits opposite me on a glass chair positioned on
the other side of an irregular-shaped raw edged drift-
wood table. *Desperately need something to calm my queasy.*
I try to keep pesky thoughts at bay, but they hound me
all the same. *Ask her, ask her, ask her.*

She pours lemonade for us. *Ask her, ask her, ask her.*

Silence fills the breathing space until I choke out, "Your
house is an amazing shape – like a giant garlic clove."

"Yes, thank you." She responds in dulcet undertones,
"yes, it was intentional." Then an awkward silence be-
falls us. We feign ease, until finally,

she advances, "Curio. All the flowers you see here
are hermaphrodite flowers, all of them have both male
and female reproductive organs within the same flower."

"Sometimes referred to as perfect flowers," I say.

"Yes," she says, "you know that. Are you interested
in botany?"

"A little," I say, "the science of things, and I love
the idea that fish are androgenous forms."

"Me too. You know, my late partner was also moved
by the breath of twinship."

The tension in the room loosens, grows less taut
as we begin to adjust to one another – looking in,

looking in. *Why am I so curious about what might
hurt me?*

She says, "I call this place The Clove. Built it with
my own two hands, from reclaimed materials
found on this domain, the lands of Sweven."

"It's amazing," I respond to keep things flowering,
"Sweven is an interesting name, I've never heard
the word before."

After a thoughtful silence she responds – carefully
considering each word, she says, "Sweven means,
a dream... or a vision seen in sleep."

OMG! It's her! My mind starbursts. Grip the arms
of my chair with my fingertips so I don't blast off.

She continues her underwater ballet, sculling
as she speaks, "but as you already know, dreams
were outlawed long ago. Teach a person to dream,
and..."

Whose side is she on? OMG! She works for the DOD!
It was a huge mistake to come here.

Je fuse – tu fuses – elle fuse – nous
fusons – vous fusez – elles fusent.

Burst. Don't burst. *I'm roiling! Hear the sound,*
stellar waves coiling just before the explode supernova.

My brain's about to detonate. Grip! Grip! Grip!
How did I end up here? When will she disappear me?

Sketchy ideas!

Don't know who I am anymore, almost as though
my being has been taken over by another person.
Possession? I'm doing things I've never done before,
never dreamed of, thought of. Everything's wobbly,
living in a lemonade haze. Act normal. *Unquestionable
questions. No speculations, deductions.* Exact science.
Make a theory. Disprove it! Right!

The aquatic Oneironaut allowed me a brief glimpse
into Sweven, starting with The Clove. *Why do that
if you're a DOD spy?* Right.

O's dream dwelling bulb is in fact a living, breathing
abode – a being with personality, moods, opinions.
Act normal. Be pedestrian. State the obvious.

I postulate, "The backwall of your sanctum sanctorum
faces due east and it's embedded with crystals."

"Yes, it isn't," she responds, her seaweed hair ripples,
"it's a net of jewels and every crystal jewel reflects all
other jewels, as we look inside the fractal mind of Indra."

"There's a sunrise in each crystal within a crystal. It's a wall
of daybreak glass turning into spinning dawn prismatic,
fractal fantastic." *Did I just say that? Out loud? Or did I
say it inside my head?* The infinite mirror casts millions
of reflections all over the floor.

O turns illusionist, to reveal, "living in each bead crystal
is an unsuspected world... a sephiroth in the tree of life.
They deflect negative spirits, and they send spells back
to their source."

"I... see... " I think, either she's a malevolent witch
or a terrifying giant fish.

Luckily the music of Mandelbrot kicks in
$$[Zn+1 = Zn^2 + C]$$

audio visual   the room turns   dichroic   it turns
    cosmic acoustic   chromatic   hypnotic
  incalculable   mathematical   it turns
       caustic   fractal fantastical
    impossible   colours per   particle shelling
    self-replicating   oscillating   intricate
images   patterns   light
    dancing   the space   under-
  water   spiraling   oceanic
    aquatic   caustic   quadratic,

filled with joie de vivre, the bulb bubbles over, rife
with life. The Clove almost giggling. *PING!* Sending
us intergalactic messages in twirling asymmetrical
mandalas.

The Clove's an extension of O and her sorcery as light
whirls us infinitely dervish. Sipping lemonade. The root
vegetable abode chaînés into trance, waltzing us deeper
underwater. We are radiantly enhanced, immersed in
many dimensions all at once,

we're in the aquarium of another aquarium of another
aquarium, waltzing essence imaginarium, she across
from me. We, in the centre of a moving marine museum
swimming with exotic Pisces light.

I deflect the ogling eyes of O. The fish stop for an instant,
scrutinize us from outside the glass. We're their research
subjects.

O shots me a noumenon smile, and says, "Curio, the fish
want to know more about you."

SQUAWK! An iridescent Macaw dive-bombs my head, does a circular sweep of the room. It's plumage so bright it looks colour enhanced – cobalt blue mixed with lime green – back feathering wings. It has a canary yellow nape breast ring, scarlet red neck and legs with a long draping tail of flames. I'd say, arial bioluminescence.

O snicker-speaks, "Don't worry, that's just Nuance. He's a free flying parrot and a bit of a nut and spirit nuisance but he won't hurt you unless you piss him off. Then he can turn goliath gryphon."

SQUAWK! Nuance stammers, "Pretty bird, petty bird. You're the one who's crackers!" He lands on a tree-like perch in a rounded side-room filled with creatures.

O catches my curiosity, and introduces the other animals as if they're human, "Perceval, Bruadar, Aisling... this is Rain."

They lift their heads in unison as if they understand, as she resumes, they each give me a nod, "Perceval's the Lilac Point Siamese with deep blue eyes in his spot on the tapestry pillow. Bruadar's the short-haired noir Bombay, sploot on the windowsill. And dear Aisling's the Golden Chausie with green eyes who's yawning."

Am I under the influence? An awkward sensation arises when I wave at them, and they smile.

O interrupts, "Don't know where Sphinx Helena is, but then again, I never do."

"I've never seen so many pets!"

"Thank the breeder, Zemis, our resident veterinarian. Allow me to introduce the dogs, Violet and Shumba... Violet's a Newfoundland and Shumba's a Rhodesian Ridgeback.

And then there's Ralphie the Reptile, but he's nocturnal... only comes out at night. You need night-vision goggles to see him."

"A reptile?!"

"He's a prehensile monkey tail skink."

Squeamish, I get the heebie-jeebies at the thought a skink is skulking.

O is on a roll, "and for comic relief there's a Creep of Geckos on the loose. There's Echo Gecko, Blotto Gecko, Sando Gecko, Deco Gecko, Falsetto Gecko, Speedo Gecko, Libido Gecko, Neat-o Gecko, and Gary... who doesn't think he's a gecko at all."

Snort! I laugh my apples off! *Good-bye cookie-cutter world! Hello astral mammals, avions, and reptiles.*

Outside the window, a pride of peahens and cocks sashay back and forth, busy doing the gardening ?¿ ?¿ ?¿ ?¿ ?¿?¿?¿

Rain's Data Log
Private Notes XVI – Subliminal Euphoria

Hours stream by in slow motion on speed.
O and I move from lemonade to sweet hot tea
and from hot sweet tea to chilled honeybee
wine.

She pours mine, and says, "this wine is from
my wildflower honey reserve. We put a gold
bee on the label to remind us it's much more
potent than it appears."

What does that mean? Who's 'we'? Sip, sip, sip,
"delish," the gold wildflower honeybee wine
fractals my mind, branches it out – skewers
my vision slightly.

Am I seeing things? Did I just see an evanescent
streak? Was it an apparition?¿ ?¿ ?¿ ?¿ ?¿?¿?¿
No! No! It's the gold bee label wildflower honey
reserve, silly.

If I believed in ghosts, I'd say it was a ghost,
but I don't believe in ghosts. *Right! Not a ghost.*
But everything's changing, notably everything
I thought I believed in. *Vroom!*

Shivers shudder up my spine. Don't know what
to say, so I don't say a thing. Sip, sip, sip the gold
bee label wildflower honey reserve till my tongue
unties, till it gives me the nerve to speak to O,

"Thing is... I'm here... yes, here... I'm... here...
wondering..."

"Yes...?"

"If you'd be willing to... speak to me... about being an Oneironaut... and... dream healing."

A long uncomfortable hiatus transpires.

"Why do you think I'm an Oneironaut?"
Her mermaid hair catches the light, wavers
fish scale – colours of the spectrum.

"I don't. I mean not for sure... sure, like I...
don't know anything for sure... anymore,
like if Oneironauts are Unicorns."

"Why do think I'm an Oneironaut?" She lifts
one eyebrow.

"I... found an article about you in... an old
Scientific Now magazine, in a banned second-
hand bookstore." Sip, sip.

She blurts out, "That damn article," then dials
it back, "almost cost me my life."

All the air gets sucked from the room. I want
to die, but say, "I'm sorry, I didn't mean to...
find it. I stumbled upon it, but when I touched
the magazine... I felt alive for the first time in
my life. Like I was meant to find it, and you."

A long pause. Heavy deliberations stockpile
until the room's filled with an unbearable
emotional hoard.

Still, neither of us will blink.

My eyes over the lip... sip... sip. *What lies
between us right now is the opposite of a click.*

Nuance breaks our deadlock. *SQUAWK!*
"Spin three times, spit, and curse, then knock
under the table thrice, to be allowed back in..."

Automatonlike O stands up and spins on the spot,
then she spits an, "F-bomb blitz," sits back down,
knocks the bottom of the table three times, then
pulls my alarm, "looking beyond darkness into
inner consciousness. What's your true interest
in extreme dream?"

Strung out by the unusual display of superstition
and open thaumaturgy I clarify, "Desperate people
commit desperate acts, and I'm already quailing,
having committed a rash of insurrections against
the regime. I don't know why, but everything I've
learned has led me here." I quiver inside. My body
turns jellyfish. Stars, stars seeing stars. *Must be the
honeybee wine. On the brink of passing out.*

Winded I say, "Don't know if I can go back to X-
City," wheezing, "there's nowhere to hide, not
even from myself, or especially not from myself."
Severe sensation as drowning.

Hang onto the table, to stabilize, "Since I stopped
taking the MetaNoia... it's like I've been called, or
pushed... pulled... tossed around. *OMG!* I can't
explain why I vaporized my entire life!"

Instant lacrimation! But not with a gradual
escalation, no, this kickstarted at ten of a total
meltdown – tears spitting from my eyes.

O comforts me, "Oh my dear," she wraps herself
around me, "sorry, I've spent years mistrusting
everyone from the outside world. Now I can see
you're genuine, and of course I'll help you learn
about O-nauts."

I lift my head slowly, O's Clove is underwater
through my tears.

She adds the absurdity, "Phases are always better
than stages. Have no fear of the depths but
always dread the shallow waters."

What... ?

Her eyes burn a biologic reaction into my skin,
"You say you're a scientist, tell me about that."

Did I mention that? "Well, I was a scientist of sorts
but more like a lab rat in the service of the DOD."

"Really?"

"Not directly, more indirectly. I don't know what
made me quit and lead me to find the *SciNow* mag,
but since then, I've been whisked away in the land-
slide of perplexity."

In a suspicious tone she asks, "Does the DOD know
about this?"

"Yes and no. I received DOD funding for a spurious
project in which I told them I'd research the genome
script, the language of nucleotides, and then develop
an algorithm for the optimization of genomic control."

"Wow!"

"I submitted a convincingly irresolvable project
to allow me to work on the real project which
I'm dubbing Oneironaut Ø1, cause it's the first
study of its kind and for all intents and purposes
the Oneironaut does not exist."

Guttural guffaw, she bubbles over in a laughter
timbre almost impossible to put into words
                    [1.5–6 kHz Speculative]

similar to a chorus of pacific tree frogs, and she
says, "Nought sure about that!"

"I lied, and told them I was studying menticide
in order to survive and study my real subject...
you and extreme dream."

"How do I know... you're not lying to me now?
You could call it Oneironaut dot naut-naut-naut
one!" She emits an ultrasonic chirp-like laugh
                    [50 kHz Empirical]

not unlike a giddy rat, adding, "it might be closer
to the truth."

No idea what she's talking about, as she continues,
"I'll agree to work with you, but with one proviso,"
she lifts her pointer finger for emphasis, "before we
begin, you must learn to dream and lucid dream."

THUD! The danger dawns on me, my heart drops
through my belly and out the bottom of my soul!
Ouch! Don't want to say yes. Don't want to say no.
I reply, "I'll... try... but I don't think I can. I'm not
a Nox Chieftain, let alone an O-naut."

"We'll see about that, Rain. Just saying, you arrived
and were able to access Sweven without a glitch
for a reason. And oh, one more thing..." she sounds
like a ventriloquist with her lips pressed to the sea-
green crystal goblet and talking at the same time,
"in the near future I may request your assistance
which I'm not at liberty to discuss at this moment..."

I hate it when people do that. I'm taken aback, no,
thrown for a loop, my voice breaks, "okay... ?"
"Sorry to set you up. This is not a quid pro quo
situation. You'll find out what I'm talking about
in due course. Please know this is for your safety.
I'm asking you to trust me."

Before I have time to ponder, she continues, "this
serendipitous meeting was prophesized."

*What!? Her words are almost completely drowned out
by my exploding brain decibels.*

Long scratchy pause.

She leans in, looks me square in the eyes, "Didn't
know how you'd come, according to the forecast
divination of Rain. But now I see the estuary point
where waters meet, and..."

Time stops. The weird apparition floats by again,
O senses it, transfixed. *Cripes!*

"Rain," she exclaims, snap me back slingshot,
"if you become extreme, we could dream
together and discover the path of Asklepios."

What! "Asklepios!" *Dream together!* I jump out
of my skin into the Athenian vision where I was
Hygieia, twin of Asklepios. *Was that a dream?
Did I just have a dream? Is this a dream right now?
My mind reels sewing machine.*

Sip, sip, sip. Buzz, buzz, buzz.

She claps her hands, CRACK, I snap back elastic,
her eyes illuminate mauve pupils – with intense
sadness, almost crushing, "Are you willing to go
to possible depths of destruction for this?"

I want to say yes, but I can't speak. I'm a storm,
chasing my own ominous cloud. *A cumulonimbus*
is building inside me, spiraling cyclonic, a violent
twister rages eyewall in my solar plexus. Neuro-
divergent, I stutter, "I... c... c... an...'t... t... ry."

"That's all I ask," she murmurs in tones typically
saved for last words.

My mind wonders, it wanders within the pelagic
expanse of else-where-ness – reminds me of being
put under – sedation – 10, 9, 8... travelling free
of the body, and,

when I come to The Clove is filled with lit candles
flickering light fantastic. *Whoa.* Guess I was talking
unaware, neither here nor there, zoned out,

'cause when I come to – O and I are half-down,
half-up – either going to stand or going to sit,
we head toward the door
                scent of lilacs spirituous-ly
                                  poignant.

A sigh of grief, I avow, "I'm leaving with much
more than I came with." Then I stun my own
stupidity with a cattle prod, "it was an honor
to meet you."

Light bends into distorted dimensions of liquid
lensing, a visible underwater window wave Snell
hallucination. I didn't drink that much, surfacing,
"I'll return to Sweven when I'm able to extreme
dream."

The Oneironaut floats in front of me, hair splayed,
we could be underwater – convex vision, looking
through a fisheye lens, she pulses, "Adieu, Rain.
It's been a pleasure. Sweet dreams." *Is she for real?*

She adds, "From now on when you think or even speak about dreaming, never use the word dream."

"What should I use?"

"Use the word, 'fish.'"

"Go figure!" I waver to my car through twilight caustics, woozy and drunkish. Everything's alive, *no,* more alive somehow. I stop, touch the trunk of the Ruin for balance, then uncharacteristically stand perfectly still to listen to the silence.

For the first time in my life, I hear beyond sound. No, beyond silence, a mythical person living in perpetual mist, near the land of the dead. Meta-physically charged.

Everything tingles. The enviro speaks to me. Pine needles reach up and tickle the bottom of my feet.

Eventually I find the driver's seat, start the motor, turn to wave good-bye to O.

Somehow, it's already dark. The Oneironaut's gone. Can't even see a silhouette of The Clove. *Is everything an illusion? Where am? Am I?*

Don't want to return to the so-called real world. Don't have a choice, already crossed that river, devoiced.

Shift into drive. *SNAP! What magnificent trickery!* The Pearl appears. I steer into the liminal flux of the Ovoid. *Hit by the wind of deception.*

Hold onto space. *Don't fall into the vortex.* Drive down the endless driveway into ominous darkness.

The Pearl doesn't emit, absorb, or reflect light, *again,* making it invisible. Drive down the tunnel guided by the unknown. Hold on. *Hold on.*

Again, temporal ambiguity.

SNAP! Exit Transdimensional Portal.

On the other side of the Ovoid Pearl,
I put the car in park, turn off the engine,
and fall asleep in the front seat. *Ruin feels
like a friend.* Does not.

Je pêche – tu pêches – elle pêche – nous pêchons... zzz... vous pêchez... zzz...

elles... pêchent...

Nuance, I say, come here dear. Let me look
into your eyes. They say the eyes of a parrot
are the mirror to the pneuma.

SQUAWK! Pneuma! No! No! I can't breathe!
I'm not going to be your prophet puppet!

Sorry, Nukey, just trying to unravel things
stringing me out!

K! K! Look into my eyes to see yourself. Ear
holes open. I'll listen 'til I can't anymore.

The cry of the sea inside me has intensified,
crashing against my inner cliffs. When I looked
into Rain's eyes – timelapse fast-forward – I saw
the very shadow I'm hiding from skulking there.

SQUAWK! Projecting! You're projecting!

No. I saw the darkness that lives inside me
living inside her, and it was ominous.

SQUAWK! If she's the tempest! You're Miranda!

Williwaw! If I hit instant replay and slow every-
thing down, to frame-by-frame. If I stretch time,
taffy-like, her shadow is a riot, a rolling squall.
She peels into a skyquake filled with ghosts
about to strike from her raven skies.

Nuance beaks off with, stop with the metaphors
already, you're making me dizzy, I'll plunge off
my perch!

Okay. Sorry.

CLICKCLICK! Rain is to it as I am to a cassowary.
SCREECH! Beautifully deadly! He flaps his wings
for punctuation, not locomotion.

I answer, she's more than a cloud. Seriously stewing
and brewing, about to burst.

CLICKCLICKCLICK! Like a fart?! *SQUAWK!*

Nuance!

CLICKCLICKCLICK!

Today may change her story, and mine, and ours.
I saw into her pent-up thunderhead just before
she lets one rip!

SQUAWK! HOOT! SHRIEK! SHRIEK! SHRIEK!

You sound like a bonobo being tickled.

SQUAWK! I'm echoing you. That's how you sound
when you laugh, like an ape being tickled! He lashes
out, you need to fish, Lily! You need to fish phantastic!
Stop being vexed by your father's hex! *CLICKCLICK!*
Leave the dreadful seizure behind. You need to stop
thinking with your mind. *CLICKCLICK!* Think with
your whole being, being, whole being.

You're right!

Right! Right! You're bloody well right, I'm right!
Think with your body-mind. Body-mind umbra,
uber umber Lily. Let go of time – there's no time
like now. *SQUAWK!* And judgements, no self-sab.
No shoulda, coulda, woulda's – all woulda coulda
shoulda's begone. *CLICKCLICKCLICK!*

Here, Nukey, let me rub your sweet spot! *PURR...*
You sound like an old lady who smoked too much,
when I rub your neck, you purr like a cat. *PURR...*
PURR... I purr back to him and whisper, thanks
for that reecho putty cat. *PURR...* Wonder if heady
Rain will be able to reach into her spirit and slow
herself down enough to raise her frequency level
to that of lucidity. I wonder if she can lose control
enough to reach into powerlessness. *PURR...*
You sound like Aisling right now.

Do I? *PURR...* Sometimes it's hard to remember
who I am under my parrot feathers! And I wonder
if you're speaking about Rain, or yourself? Rain,
or yourself. Rain, or yourself. Who's personating
whom? O, there, there you go! There! There! Keep
on rubbing there! O yeah... sweet tweet, you got
the magic spot, the magic spot, the magic spot,
spot, spot. *SQUAWK!*

Okay, I kiss Nuance on the crest of his abalone
beak,

then I cross the room to the driftwood shelf,
talking to myself, which notebook did I write
it in? Which one has the motherload?

Scan, scan... oh yes, here it is!

I open the journal labelled #246, *Mind Bending
Flip Book*, down its spine. Scan, scan.

Eye shock. It's hard to see all the knowledge
I once knew by rote. *Dream Notes,* from the days
of yore – another lifetime ago.

FLIPFLIPFLIP flicker book style, and in the *FLIP-
FLIP* flow, the pages stop on an old info dump.

My eyes snag on the karmic thread of dread
as I reexplore the hurt of lost Hz written in
a teenage hand, overly swirly and curvaceous.

1 Hz = 1 wave passing a fixed point/second

Low (< 500)	Hear and Feel
Medium (500-2,000)	Tinny Horn-like Quality
High (2,000 >)	@10,000 Bird Chirps
4-8 Hz	Lucid Dreaming (Theta waves)
8 Hz	Binaural Beat Brainwaves
	Frequency of Nightmares/ LD
25-40 Hz	Brain Zap
40 Hz	Reverses Alzheimer's in mice
111 Hz	Holy Frequency (induces LD)
174 Hz	Tones in Sacred Music, Alt Medicine
432 Hz	Astral Realm/Cerebral Music/
	Opens 3rd Eye
528 Hz	Miracle Tone
963 Hz	Pure Miracle Tone
62-78 MHz	Overall Range of Human Body
72 MHz	Normal Brain
80-82 MHz	Genius Brain
58 MHz	Disease starts at
25 MHz	Death begins at

I love the me of then as I'm taken back to when
I wanted to try everything and anything. Nothing
could stop me, not even my father's stringent rules
or unattainable ambitions. Not even his inability
to see me, acknowledge me, accept me. He knew,
yet look what he did.

What happened to her? What happened to that little
girl so filled with big ideas and enormous fish? What

happened to her? *FLIPFLIPFLIP* back to the time
I followed my heartbeat, rhythm of torn stars
when I danced to the beatitude of my own wyrd.

FLIPFLIPFLIP must return to my naïve essence.
First-time eyes. Must return to the reason I fished
in the first place, instinct whimsy with no reason.

Yes, back to the beginning when I fished to escape,
FLIPFLIP play in hidden places. *FLIP* into the flow
of recovery *FLIP* into discovery *FLIP* emancipated
from the addlepated and constipated. It's time to
throw anchors to the wind and rebegin again. Yes,
it is, Nuance.

You got this Lilly-Billy-Boo! *SQUAWK!*

Come 'ere, honeybunny! He lands on my shoulder,
and I tell him, when I was a kid teachers and spirit
guides, decagons of the wise came to me in visions
and fish. *FLIPFLIP* look, they fill these pages.

CLICKCLICK! Grab your rod, dig some worms.
Let's go fishing! Fishing! Let's go fish-ing-ing-ing!

My mind reels, tries to comprehend the day Che
was taken away, ripped from our world. That day
I was stripped of my true love and my Oneiro-naut,
in one blow – we both disappeared – in one swift
strike of the grim reapers scythe, I was left to walk
the yellow line of the bone causeway alone.

SQUAWK! Alone! You sound like a piece of twisted
wood washed up on the beach after a storm. *EEK!*
Crackers!

Sorry Nuance, you're right. You've been with me
every dunk and slam of the choppy seas. I am not

alone, but I need to know what lies underneath
the shadow of that fateful day.

CLICKCLICKCLICK! Yes, you do driftwood!
First find that impossible frequency Lily, the 111
one hidden away, locked inside a witch's bridle
mask of shame. You're tortured! SQUAWK!

Yes, I know, I live beside the ocean, and still
I long for the sea! All I fish is to have a fishing
fantasy. The taste of salt licks me – it tempts
me to dive in, but I can't for fear the waves
of grief pull me under.

You can't give up! Find the key! Be free. Swim
the waters of Dwam again! Breathe! Breathe!

You're right Nuance, I know myself better now.
I'm more adept, able to pass the tests of darkness
again, to regain the nauts I lost when my memory
was wiped.

SHRIEK! Return to the light! Whip-poor-will-o-
the-wisp-o-whip-poor-will-o-the-wisp. SQUAWK!
You're one in a mill!

Did you say, run of the mill?

No, one in a mill! A mill! Million. Absolute!
Infinitesimal! SQUAWK! Time to speak again!

For most of my life I thought I was the only one,
till I met Che and realized others like me existed,
however rare. Nukey, not sure I have the strength,
but I'll try to reach the frequency, listening in for
the ecstatic flow – 111 – the astral chartography.

Cosmology! You got this Lily pad!

WAGGAWAGGA!
Place of many crows.

Pandemonium. *CLICKCLICK!*

Pod. Must allow my brain to change dominance
left-to-right,

then activate the lucid fish state that penetrates
the 9th chakra,

that will assist in the shift. Must zap the jade pillow
alive.

SQUAWK! Yes! Cross the bridge! The bridge! Activate
the Soul Star!

Rain's Data Log
Private Notes XVII – Re: turn to Re: ality

Dawn light breaks through the red cedars, lands
square on my eyes, blinks me out of moonshadow
into rise and shine.

So far, I've stayed two nights outside the gates
of Sweven, *tee-hee,* The Hubcap Hotel!

Part of me wants to stay here forever, the other
part wants to run away, never to return.

Part of me wants it to stop, return to the old
normal, whatever that is. The other part wants
to use chronokinesis, turn back time, return to
the bookshop and never pick up the *SciNow.*

Omnium immanent.

I roll down the windows, recline back, breathe
in the morning freshness, light and trees, green
nibbana. I breathe in the triumph of finally
finding O.

Dawn turns aurora into day. *Dang!* I try to get
my bearings, heart racing, don't want to move,

still, I leap out, toss the hubcap – LM + Crown
in the backseat and begin my drive back to X-City,

immediately scanning for surveillance eyes,
expecting to die at any moment.

I wish the black Pearl would appear, but nada.

Hiraeth means longing for home. *Do I?* I have
my own personal nameless grey zone, lodger

in an unmarked grave. No headstone.
It's time to change – to find out who I am, beyond
what I knew – biweekly paychecks, picking bones.

Stick to the backroads, my mind-bends, merges
with unfamiliar moods – turns around altered
points of view.

Mermaids have a reputation of being terrifying
but they're nothing compared to the DOD.

Exhilarated, I carve in and through curvy roads,
zigzag cosmic race car, zinging idea-to-idea,
where's the Pearl?

Why isn't the Pearl appearing?

"Ovoid, Ovoid, calling all Ovoids. Appear now
or forever hold your cockatrice."

Who am I?

Agitated. Pacing around The Clove, wearing
a path line in the floorboards and carpets.

The door opens. Jet walks in. Lines blur.
As she speaks her physique oscillates between
her blood-red fire snake and her human self.

Sorry to pull you away from the lab, I say,
thanks for making time.

Of course, her voice doesn't vary as she adds
from her snake self, no problem my friend,
from her human self she asks, what happened?

Rain showed up at dawn as you predicted, I say,
but she didn't fall from the sky as I projected, no,
this Rain arrived in the form of a person.

Intriguing. Snake, human, snake, human.
Jet doesn't seem surprised. She reveals
an aspect of herself I've never seen.

I nervously continue, somehow this Rain person
found the disastrous article from ages ago when
they outed me as an Oneironaut and pushed me
underground... as a dissident... along with you,
Che, and the other Nox Chieftains. That was back
before we knew there were more than one O's.

Jet, snake, Jet, snake, Jet, oh, I see...

This Rain seems to know I'm the O in the article,
I say, she was able to track me down, long and lat
to here. Can't believe anyone could break through
our firewalls, but she did – she just rolled in like
she'd rolled in a million times before.

Not good.
What do we do?

Her snake red grows redder, she asks,
where is she now?

She returned from whence she came.

Oh no, Lily, you let her leave, Jet exclaims,
Is she going back to X-City?

I confess, I forgot to ask where she lives,
but I assume so.

Well, what did she want?

To learn more about O-naut powers
and dream healing.

Achcha! She flips skin to scale, scale to skin, rapid
fire till they appear as one. One of two, two of one.

After a moment she slows down and says, it's all
good, I'll figure it out.

I go on, thank-q. I told her before anything happens,
first, she must become a lucid dreamer. I thought it
would buy us time to figure this out. Oh, and then
I told her, after she becomes lucid, she can return to
Sweven. I didn't know what else to say – it caught
me off-guard, and we were drinking gold.

Jet's expression turns to deep concern. Achcha!
It's alright. It's all good. Problem is, as you know,
once a person becomes a lucid dreamer, the gates
of their consciousness open...

... subconsciousness, you mean...

... yes, and then all Oneiroi will break loose.
Oh no... and I told her to replace the d-word
with the f-word.

What?

Fish!

We laugh like a couple of giddy teen-agers,
and high-five one another!

Jet resumes, when a person starts unravelling
who they really are, it can be mega-over-whelming,
and if they're a born dreamer, with the blood...
of an O... or NC... well, you remember...

What should we do?

First, Rain needs to be protected. If she dreams
and The Bureau picks up the intel, she's toast.
Not to mention... when they're finished polishing
her off, their taste for blood revived, they'll likely
hunt us all down like the predators they are.

Oh no... yes... right... no...

We need to test her DNA somehow. Did you happen
to get anything we can sample?

Proudly I proclaim, thought you'd ask, so, I bagged
her mug. And you're not going to believe this, but
when she was here, she got a nosebleed.

What!? Who gets nosebleeds?

Her.

How convenient is that! Good work, Lily, that
should do the trick. I'll weave a protective spell
to cloak her in the Ovoid.

Thank-q, Jet.

She becomes her writhing snake self, firebird red,
in a continuous empyrean undulation, hiss-hiss,
I'll send her a telepathic message instructing her
to write her notes in invisible ink.

Oldest trick in the book!

Hiss-hiss, it works, 'cause they don't suspect it.
Don't know why, it reminds me of the old adage,
if you drive a stick-shift you're safe, your car will
never get stolen ∵ no one knows how to drive
a stick anymore.

SSS SSS SSS   Kookaburra cackle   *SSS SSS SSS*
Kookaburra   *SSS SSS SSS*   Cackle *SSS SSS*

After a bout of laughter, a frisson of fear
and excitement coulombs between us.

Oh! Says Jet, I'll also increase security for you,
the Willows and all Sweven. Times are changing.
Let's hope we can change with them, reverse
the curse and return to the good old days,
the ancient ways.

Yes, Jet.

I've got your back, Lily, we all do.
Lucky, we don't live in a silo!

Thank-q. Thank-q for everything.

Of course. Jet smiles slyly, yo-yoing
between her selves, before she splits
in a wisp.

Rain's Data Log
Private Notes XVIII – Re: turn to Re: ality 2

Onboard a Stone Age ferry, on the top deck
on the lookout for autocratic eyes – never
been on a ferry before,

this one must serve rebels living on the out-
side realm,

out of sight, sleight of mind, my mind, *or is it?*
Dido that. *Cripes! How did I get here?*

I drift into quietude – bird-like fish-like – drift,
into the wind, into the middle, to the betwixt
of between, terminals and time intervals. I spiral
into the limbo that mixes awake and asleep.
Hypnagogia hypnotizes me.

Weird to be in the unauthorized world, solone,
following the contour line on a real-time paper
map, *flash on isobar option.* Only I'm voyaging
across the water at who knows how many knots
an hour. It's uncharted – all I see ahead of me
is open blue ocean – a mermaid's milieu – O...

I stand perfectly still in a trance. Watch the light
shimmer along the surface of the sea spectacular,
reflection, an oceanic murmuration. It soothes me
as a lover – as the sea meets the sky, it looks me
in the eye. It fills a void inside me. *What gives?*
Is this poetry hour? Whoa!

Haven't thought of love in ages – didn't know
I could. *What's happening?*

Close my eyes. *Sigh.* Breathe the boundless sea air
into my lungs. *Sigh.* Inside my eyes I glide, skim

the surface of timelessness. Exteroception stimuli
extrasensory as wind blows my hair, erect.

My mind expands into infinity. All thoughts leave.
Something lifts from my being. I tingle all over
like when I was a child.

Cognitive chaos – thought scramble – lost brother –
Asklepios – Hygieia – Oneironaut – Sweven –
a single hubcap – Nox Chieftains – the Pearl.
Whoa! The Department of ~~Dreams~~ Fish – *hahaha!*

Waves of rage rush through me, WHOOSH,
all things taken away. The lies, wring out secrets
behind my eyes, in the theatre of my mind, a play,
tragedy of circumstance, overarching betrayal
runs again and again, in my hippocampus hippo-
drome – which activates an existential shattering.

Time dilation, unfathomable. Standing on deck
in the heat of a new summer sun—

may be experiencing thermodynamic improbability,
floating on an Oort cloud,

> *Oort cloud*
> *Oort.*

Umpteenth temporal flux. Open eyes.

Look around. There's no one here, no one
watching. Alone, all alone. The sole survivor.

Free for the first time in my life to experience
nothing beyond the experience itself, *experiential
void,* and therefore the nature of all existence.

The Absolute. The Nameless Reality. *Whoa!*
This is probably what life spice feels like.
What? What am I thinking? I'd never do drugs.
Then again, why do drugs if there's this.

The wind wafts – makes chaos of my hair,
sensate it, standing on end – faux-hawk-ish.

Imagine I look cool for once. *Doubt it.*
Wince at the thought.

My mind wanders meta-awareness *[fMRI],*
perceptual decoupling.

I'd like to be tough as a micro-badass Tartigrade,
little water bear,

then I'd be able to survive anything, even exposure
to outer space. I love Tartigrades a tun! *A tun!* A tun!
That's it! The key! Cryptobiosis! The protective state
of the black Ovoid Pearl, same as the Tartigrade tun!
Love their otherworldly noses!

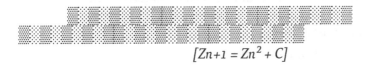

$$[Zn+1 = Zn^2 + C]$$

A letter to O forms in my mind...

DEAR OCEANID O

Can't believe I found you
                      spent the whole day
           on the other side with you
      it was astro-nautical
       high $[(x^2 + y^2 + ax)^2 = a^2(x^2 + y^2)]$

            chimerical   aero-alchemical

            untying   metaphysics of make

believe   real   & un
                                                    real
                clouds can hide

    you with   me & me   with you

        dangerous   tripwires   inside

    you're a radical   dream fish

            I   an outsider   in

    despair   I've always been

DEEP   REM

there, repeating myself in the quantum corridor
never followed my intuition, never had an eleven
of ambition.

But it's a new game, different rules. *I've been touched
by the enzyme of destiny,* a predetermined trajectory.
The DOD earworm that lobotomized me has been
removed from my mind.

There's something about you I can't put my finger
on. You make me dream fish of the ocean, maybe
∵ you're of the sea. Please forgive my hypothesis
if it's off key, my Oceanid naut, Oneiro esprit.

MEWMEWMEW! Sound from the outside, from out-
side my head – my body, mind. Won't open my eyes,
scared I'll lose the thought thread! *DEAR O*

I've entered a space where time is beyond time itself *chrono-cosmical*, replete in a vacuum with an unwonted sense of optimism. Devoid of devoid. *Hope the daemons* that haunt me day-in night-out, waking and sleeping *will deliquesce back to their slimy cesspool*, so I can focus on ~~dreaming~~ fishing.

MEW! MEW! MEW! Saltwater air blows through my body, my being – 'til I no longer exist. *Must stay inside the sandbox. DEAR O*

Always felt like an outsider, but I towed the line following orders – obedient – every step – killing time – in a life empty – of questioning – settling for compliancy, mediocrity. But I was always out of step, which is likely why I always had a bloody nose or a stubbed toe – always running into walls.

I'm beginning to think when we swallow the pill the friggin' DOD enters our consciousness, no, subconsciousness and then we simultaneously consume and are consumed by their cacotopia. *Incipient clarity...*

When I say 'their,' I mean them – that tyrannize, the authorities. Strange, I know nothing about 'them,' and yet I obeyed them to the nth degree, *how somnambulant is that?*

Must learn everything about the 'them.' Spent my life on the suburbs of my good conscience, & now it's time to return from the tun, from life without H_2O to aqueous-ence ?¿ ?¿ ?¿ ?¿ ?¿?¿?¿ Maybe I'm a micro-badass Tartigrade after all!

Still I shutter, scared stiff of DOD as their utter tyranny. Their imperious soundbites replay in my mind, 'If you're caught, you'll be shot.'

Welcome to slogan city! It's not demonstrators
hollering, but a regime, quietly whispering a deadly
catchphrase into your ear every time you move,
press conference after press conference:
'Traitors, violators, and all collaborators
will not be tolerated. They will be terminated,
and their families eliminated.'

Disinformation. Authentic Authoritarian!
Depopulation. Elimination of all opposition.

Buried alive. I'll be stripped of my identity, *though
when did I last exist?* I'll be divested of all security,
they have the authority. My personal effects will be
seized, appropriated. Out of nowhere, my voice
will be removed, my vocal cords cut by a serrated
blade. I'll be asphyxiated. Silenced. Expunged.

A plastic bag held down over my head. Hypoxia
is loss of consciousness, brain damage, then organ
failure, cyanosis, respiratory arrest, and eventually
an untimely death. There will be no scream. Blood
will drain from my body 'til I am dead.

Gasp! Open my eyes. *Wait! Maybe it's not too late!*
In Greek the word 'apocalypse' is derived from,
'a revelation.' *Senseless rambling.* Not!

Don't know what I'm doing. Fake it 'til I make
it. Reminds me of what Uncle Ed always said,
'If you look in the mirror and see the deep-fake
face of a suckafish with an ice pick in your brain,
its time to change, Rain!'

All I want is to lucid ~~dream~~ fish. Then I'll research
how fishing intersects with healing, à la Asklepios.
I know it's prohibited, but I'll take the risk. If I end
up with a sharpened screwdriver in my gut, so be it.
I will have lived.

Blinded by the sun. Close my eyes again. Resume
the monologue pretending to be a dialogue.
DEAR O

Today I was distracted and forgot to ask you what
your real name is. Based on the hubcap inscription,
LM, I'm guessing Little Mermaid. No! Just joking...

LMO, let's move on...

who cares, you can't read me right now
anyway.

Why do I see a snake with an egg in its mouth?

The DOD have eyes and spies everywhere.
Won't tell a single soul. No, getting caught
is not an option.

I'll covertly return to #303A, become
lucid, and then return to these waters,
and eventually to you and your O-naut.

Unfalteringly yours,
Rain

A voice that sounds like her whispers, "go fish."

Must be my mind playing tricks with me again.
Cool and not cool concurrently.

Breathe salt air, wind whips through my being,
sea gulls call, the ferry prepares to berth.

My plans have a domino effect – topple me over.
Overcome, my body trembles, I burst into tears.

DEEP REM

My mind blanks. Don't know why, but I flip back
to my youth. Once again inside the deathblow.

Reliving the loss of a brother I wasn't allowed to have.
No. Doing everything I was told to do by a mother
who pushed me to be normal, fit in, never stand out.
To dig my teeth into hard work, goal oriented,
practical. *To swallow the pill.* Swallow the pill.

Tears downpour over the lip of my lower eyelid
blurring my vision – underwater optical illusion.

The ocean wind lifts – blows across the top deck
– a fierce message from the sea. I surrender to
the erratic, weep wild Neptune streaks.

I can't remember the last time I sobbed. My tears
are salty aliens, and life is short – so it doesn't take
long for it to catch up with you.

Loudspeakers, 'return to our vehicles.' I pull myself
together – head down to the lower decks – atypical
environs – reverse direction – avoid cameras, divert
eyes. *CLANG-CLANG,* down metal stairs that lead
to the belly of the boat. *CLANG-CLANG,* my mind
delves into the salt-burn of my life,

pole-vaults to the first day of my so-called dream
job – the job that pushed me down the rabbit hole
of daily grind, resigned to a job I was adequate at,
CLANG-CLANG, a flatline on a graph – skivvy lab
rat – tail deep in education debt owed to the DOD.

On the last set of stairs my body buckles in lament,
crisis in keening, realizing, this is a suicide of who
I was, or who I wasn't. A waterworks of salt stings
my eyes. My body crumples like a Styrofoam cup,
it sends me off balance. I take a spill on the last

stair, barely catch myself. Grip the metal handrail.
*Wish I was a Tartigrade right now – safe in a tun state
or inside the Pearl Ovoid – blink and I'd be someplace else.*
But I'm not – nought! Instead, I'm lost in hull space.
Can't find my car. Why are there so many cars?
There are no people. *Who's driving all these cars?*
JUMP.

$$[Zn+1 = Zn^2 + C]$$

INTRA-MORPHOSIS

Asklepios appears before me apparition-like,
transparent. *I don't believe in ghosts.*

He descends from another time, says, "Follow
me." The serpent on his rod slithers, "asp, asp."
He continues, "Sister, learn to swim the waters
of fish. Trust your own blood." "Asp, asp, asp."

Next thing I know I'm sitting behind the wheel.
Am I? Other cars are honking for me to move.
I shift Ruin into drive. Jolt. *Rune.*

Enigmatic inertia strikes. I disembark spaced out,
there's a gap between dimensions of consciousness.

I click into automatic pilot. *Snake venom is used for
healing... and... killing!*

DEEP REM

Asklepios is in the passenger seat. *Did he call shotgun?*

He's mid-story, "... and then history rewrote us,
to suit itself. You were never my daughter, Hygieia.
You are, always have been, always will be my twin,
my identical twin. We always revelled in our sibling
rivalry, challenging one another into wider realms
of deeper thought. That's what we did, together
and apart. We were, and we are healing/dreaming
practitioners, sister, that's what we must do now,
in order to survive."

Sideways glance in the rear-view mirror, I gleam
a snake smiling at me, "Asp, asp." Double take.
She slithers. *Strange assumption... she.*

The snake metamorphoses between Pythia
and an unidentified woman – a gyneco-ophidian
now sits in the backseat. She gives me a thumbs up.
How is this possible?

I smile backward at her, rearview. *She gives me another
thumbs up!*

Asklepios continues, "Sister, we are few, but we are
powerful. We will anticipate difficulties and we will
try to protect you in every way."

 (δ θ γ dream end)

malletinhand   i
            slowlycircle   rim
ringggggg
                        quartz
        singing bowl   ringggg

        ringggg   holy frequencyyyy

            ringggg   111Hz

        ringggg   wave length

        ofpyramids   tombs

            pharaohs   wave

    length   standing   stone

                        hertz   phasia

        0   Hz   ringggg

    wave

                length of rings
            and

                theholy

                    spirit
                        ringgggggggggg

111 frequency quavers, zaps the groove at the back
of my neck, where my spine meets my skull, it rings
in the holy tone – vibrates stem and cord and bone.

111 frequency rings the singing bowl through
my medulla oblongata, to open my mouth
of god, the singing bowl rings, through my jade
pillow to awaken my intuition with its sound,
lightning rod. Ensoulment, so I can Oneironaut
dream again.

111 rings through me – starting at my skull line,
and shooting up my spine, divine, in a ring tone
that might free the blocks that paralyse me
from dreaming – ringing – seeing – singing
the ringing bowl of time.

The holy frequency vibrates my hippocampus
to reinitiate extreme incubation, with the magical
activation of Aum. Ring, singing bowl, ring.

Out my window the moon climbs up the night
sky, spotlight shining through from the other side.
It claws its way up the night in a kind of suffering
all its own. *RINGRINGRING.*

Hello? Lily? Hello!? Are you there? *SQUAWK!*
Is that a G# bowl I hear you playing in the dark?
CARK! Are you stargazing? Here? There? Where?

Sorry Sweet-beak, I was trying to trigger a fish.

CLICKCLICKCLICK!

Thanks Nuance, Nuisance!

SHRIEK! SQUAWK! NUMB-NUTS!

Flap, flap, flap. He flies to the round room.

I stop playing the singing bowl... it continues
ringing long after... mesmerizing reverberation...

I am a bird after a drastic downpour,
crying out, I'm alive, I'm still alive,
but I can't fly.

From the next room, Nuance scions
his squawk-talk with, fly Lily, fly!

I wanna to fish with you again, sugar
cake, I wanna fishwalk with you, yes,
yes, I do! *CLICKCLICKCLICK!*

Rain's Data Log
Private Notes XIX – Return to Reality 3

I return to my body – speeding into a hairpin
turn. *Holy crap!* Bucking Bronc Pass, a paranormal
deathtrap, and I'm navigating a torrential torrent.
Where have I been? In a fish? Inside the Ovid Pearl?

I catch a warning sign through sheets of rain,
curtains: *Caution! Watch out for falling rock!*

"Holy shit!" I vociferate! Cursing the mortal skid,
skid, side-slide rollercoaster ride, I grip the wheel
like a coconut crab, white-knuckle hydroplane.

BREAK! EERCHHH! Rattlesnake shake, screech,
squeal. Reflex burn, reckless turn – tight as terror,
I steer the veer, the veer, the veer – car battered
like a flea in a g-force windstorm. *Don't let go!*
Hang onto the road! The road! Hang onto the road!
Steer the cliff – past near! Road! 3-2-1...

Clear. Missed the abyss of death extremis by
the Plank of a Planck's Plank. *Holy shite-skeeeeee!*
Where am I?

What's going on? Slow to a crawl, try to catch
my breath, rockoon, and they are rocketing
around the inside of the car like a deflating
balloon. Spirits appear quantum quandary!

RIFT! Ancestors. *DRIFT!* Sin-eaters. *RIFT!* Myth-
keepers. *RIFT!* I am unable to verify this reality
shift. *What's going in?*

Spirits pop into Ruin Rune, they float-in adrift,

Neowise, they fill the inside of the car. *RIFT*

AFTER RIFT!
Soothsayers. *RIFT!* Oracles. *DRIFT!*

Healers and sorcerers. *DRIFT!* Once frozen
in time, now they're very much alive.

What's Neowise? *Near * Earth * Object * Wide-*
*Field * Infrared * Survey * Explorer.* Oh yeah.

CRASHSLAM! A mountain landslide caves
in outside, *holy crap,* rugged boulders fall off
their rock faces, and come crashing down in
my path, scarring, *no barring,* the pass.

As they crash-land, they transform into giants,
chiselled out of mystic stone, all around me.
Holy crap! Is this good, or bad?

The giants thunder in a candour saved for ancient
lore, and with meteorite fists, they take Grande
swipes at Ruin Rune. *I guess bad.* I duck out
of the way, even though I'm inside. *Feckin' freck!*

Swerve right, round blue rock sorrow – left, eyes
of no tomorrow – right, amber, ocher almandine.
Crikey! Always dreamed of driving like this! Now,
I'm not so sure.

Giants flank my car, my peripheral vision rear-
blinded by the sheen of their ink black shale
glare. Are things really closer than they appear
in my rear-view mirror? $[d=\sqrt{((x\_2-x\_1)^2+(y\_2-y\_1)^2)}]$

Cromlechs boom outside. *CRASHCRASHCRASH!*
But why haven't they flattened me? I scale scary cliffs
with the edges of my wheels. They say giants once

lived here. *Never believed them. Call me a minimifidian!*
Where's that friggin' black Pearl?

Inside the car aureoles spirits talk to me,
they say, "Dance Rain. Extend your body
aura until you fill the entire car and dance
a Danse Macabre with the giant bones
of stone."

They say, "Release yourself from outcome,
come what may, it will come, it will come
what may.

And when you're in that state of alteration,
in the flow of fluctuation, your cells will
rearrange themselves."

Madness inside and out.

I ascend and descend bend-after-bend, chaos
reins outside, inside windshield wipers set on
high, beat in time with my humming heart,
WHOOSH-WHOOSH
WHOOSH-WHOOSH...

Open my ears wide, to hear the music
of gods through a cosmological stethoscope,
WHOOSH-WHOOSH
WHOOSH-WHOOSH...

Inundated by antiquities, possibilities
and prophecies,
WHOOSH-WHOOSH
WHOOSH-WHOOSH...

  I shift to another realm
 close enough to dream
    I could be a surrealist.

Life a constant state in transition
in the flux is the flow
where we grow
eclipse-to-eclipse.

Unplanned Attack
ᛉᚲᛗᛏ ᛉᚾᛉᛁᛗ

(Jet chants)
Don't know what went wrong!

(AΘE)
Call them back!

(Jet)
I can't seem to!
Something's jamming us.

DEPARTMENT OF DREAMS
SECURITY INTELLIGENCE UNIT

_____*below the bottom line*_____

Lester – "Subject # 220 455 816 must be stopped. Create interference between subject and fringe rebel group – You-Know-Who! Let's get this under control!"

Shelly – "Running interference now, through Che. It seems to be working but there's only so much torture... "

Lester – "Just get the job done, and I'm going to freeze all her bank accounts, so, she won't be able to do much more damage."

❄

Do it. Don't. *Do it.* Don't. *I'm going to.*
You're not! *I'm going to.* You're not!
What have I got to lose?

This construct isn't real. Alright, I'll dance,
but I've never been good at dancing.

Statim! Chrono-zepto. I accept the dance
with stone giants – sarsen's swift me away,
after my close brush with death, I'm swept
off my feet,

'til I can dance no longer – 'til I no longer know

I'm dancing, *spinning, whirling, waltzing,*
busting megalith moves incredible,

barely perceivable, the stone giants initiate a slow-
motion fragmentation – atomization, they splinter
apart – in a genesis of awe-wonder, *wow! As they
depart they impart a message, "To move mountains
you must move with the mountains. In spiritus."*

Then they reintegrate back into their stone jigsaw
pockets. They become part of the mountain once
more, vanishing one-by-one – they disappear,

the rain clears,

evanescent. Did it even happen? *Where am I?*
Don't care anymore, driving free of timespace,

I take to the skyway – fly through the long
syncopated tunnels – snaking through stone,
wing feather fly. I fish of fishing at 160 clicks,

ignited by change, remote and out of range
I speed towards the *CN X* nerve of deep-rooted
longing – a sense belonging.

I could do anything right now. I could follow
my lifelong fish and become a storm-chaser,
cyclone seeker,

I could hang out with other unsung misfits,
also tempest trackers in baseball caps and cool
t-shirts. And I'd live off-world with them,
away from the spying eyes of the DOD.

Maybe I'd be in Sweven – only not in this epoch!
It'd be way back when, when we were free
to chase storms – to yell over hurricane sound

waves, and tornados, and cyclones, and we'd
live-stream from dashcams, our cars decked out
with a bobble shaking hula dancers.

But I guess those days are gone ∵ climate change
has made storms ubiquitous. And we're no longer
able to chase them, tables turned, now, they're
chasing us.

What's happening to me!? This experience has hit
me like an electrostatic lightning strike, direct hit,

my mind is exploding out the top of my head,
sparks and fireworks blast from my crown
of gigajoules and stars of tempest love,

not with a strike into death
but a stroke into life.

I drive alive! I am alive!
Thank you, most wonderful world!

I've been down for the count all day, submerged
in floaters, with a head-pounding-splitter occupying
my vision with a plethora of opaque auras.

Mantis shrimp eyesight, circular rings are polarised
light refracts, bounces back – light strobe lights, disco
ball eyes. Terrible, this happens when I overdo it.

Full-body migraine, wind whirling weathervane,
nerve endings hot-wired – my head is cranked
in a dharmic vice. I'm exhausted, expired, way
past tired.

Headaches start when the jade chakra, the 9th
chakra, has closed its gates. They call it the centre
of the life force, where lucid dreams begin.

Surrounded by a myriad of doors, around, above,
below – none of them will open, no matter how
I try, I'm paralysed. Need my black dot exercise.

Black dot, find the black dot in the 3rd eye.

Black dot, find the black dot, hindsight 20/20
I misconstrued 'rain' to mean, something that falls
from the sky.

Slow my thoughts. Black, black dot – she came with
summertide, flower in full bloom – she rolled in past
our high security firewall undetected.

Black dot, change my thoughts. Black dot, heading
out to plant rutabaga – blindsided by expectation –
standing on my stoop startled as a gecko, she naively
coasted up my driveway one crunch at a time.

Stop your thoughts, think of the black dot, black dot,
she got out completely discombobulated, dishevelled,
yet handsome, she was somehow familiar.

Headache starting to close in on itself, black dot,
hold that thought. Black dot. Black dot. Stretch
the jade chakra.

Nothing could've prepared me for the intensity
of her inertia, and her movements took my breath.
Everything about her reminded me of my beloved,
my Che. My mind relaxes, a deep sigh.

Rain arrived on our anniversary, the exact day
Che and I tied the knot, twelve years ago—

the sky opened I remember it   close

            enough   to touch   the day

Che   and I   joined hands

        shared   souls   at the O stone.

Temple of the Moon
where the birds fly
                    magnetic,
                    and the sun descends
                    between tall ritual stones.

It is. It is nought.

                    At the Temple of the Moon
                    Litha day, and night,
we became two of one, and one
of two, tied by a knot, kneeling
on opposite sides of the wedlock stone.

We are. We are nought.

And the Willow prophecy—

>Reaching hands up into the night sky
>as one, their telekinesis multiplied,
>hivemind focused on riveting fingertips
>they wrangled the fiery current
>with all its tendrils
>into a single blazing sphere.

The sun is on fire.

>Rain arrived, June sun-shower flower
>of the sun, on this, the morning of the night
>of Litha when Che and I handfasted, our vows
>in the centre of stone, by day and of night,
>from dawn until dusk and dusk until dawn,
>on the day of the night of the longest light,
>fire night, turning of the light,

we joined hands, hearts, souls, in the centre
of the centre of the O stone within the stone
circle of a circle,

on the twenty-fourth day, of the sixth month,
twelve years ago today, duodecennial, we said
our vows, sealed with the kiss between ancient
obelisks – at the ancient coven stones.

<<<<<< *vena amoris* > > > > > >

Strange, I still perceive your presence.

<<<<<< *because i am here – dear* > > > > > > >

NUMEROUS CLOCKS CHIME, THEY
RING OUT IN UNISON – BONG ONE

The first strike of midnight.

BONG TWO, THREE

<<<<<<remember the knot>>>>>>

FOUR, FIVE

I wear the knots of your vows, Che.

<<<<<<our love rare as a narwhal>>>>>>>

SIX, SEVEN, EIGHT

Unicorns of the sea, and you told me
they mate for life.

NINE, TEN

We broke the ice and dove to the depths.

ELEVEN

I would crush a priceless pearl and drink it
for one last day with you.

TWELVE

I love you on this side and all others.

<<<<<<<i know you do – and i do you>>>>>>>

I do.

COO-COO, COO-COO, COO-COO

Sometimes it's like you're here talking to me.

<<<<<<<Lily of the sea-lily of the sea – in the wild
of yourself – you are everything to me – but i can't
reach you 'cause the DOD blocked your dream
ability to see me>>>>>>>

Narwhal echolocation,
will my tusk lead me to you?

Déjà reçu,
you disappeared.

Rain's Data Log
Private Notes XX – Unsettling Re: boot

Must investigate telepathy. ~~Dream~~ telepathy,
fish. Keep hearing voices. Voices in my head
that aren't my own, seriously, a new break-
through.

Made it all the way back. Don't know how,
mayhap tau. Didn't get stopped or caught,
could be my non-stop vigilance on the lookout
for surveillance.

I'm a bird returning to my rookery, *and nought,*
to the unrepeatable repeat, cognitively stochastic,
in the sweltering heat, it's impossible to repeat.

Dumped my trusty rusty Ruin Rune out of sight
so, I can return to her in the night another time,

shrewdly approach my government sponsored
housing block, which resembles the building apt
I left behind, now somehow different,

I walk down the same hallway – deadlock. Stop
at #303A, take a look at same old key, suspiciously
different today. *They should update these retro keys
to codes.*

Turn the metal key, *TICK*, the same seasick click,
but different somehow, *someone's been here, picked
this lock.* The DOD? *Do I go in or make a run for it?*
They could be inside waiting for me.

No! Something inside me's changed, lifted, shifted
I'm no longer afraid, sway, they can face my music
blaring! *Go in!* No! I can't. *Just do it!* In! Stupid
smiling face!

Should forget all of it, push reset, take my MetaNoia
Pill and forget it ever happened. *Not!* I could forget
about all of it. *No, you can't!* I've got to shake off
this billiwhack monster off my back. *Yes! Yes!*

But I'm sliding down, *whoa*, plummeting down fast,
I'm a submarine in a landslide, *dizzy*. Need to feel safe!

I should game to forget all of this for a while, yes
that'll make me feel better, *no*, go wide. *Not! Can't
do that anymore.* But can't fight the itch. I'm fiending
for game time.

Dive into something else. Can't. *Can.* Can't. *Fight old
temptations, don't return to distractions.* Can't escape
anymore. *Nothing.* Nowhere. *Unplug. Restart.* But
I've got the itch. *Kill the kill itch.*

Switch! *Change the pattern. Reconfigure your inner
algorithm. Pattern, change the pattern.* Yes, disrupt!
Perturb!

Dang! Twenty friggin' messages from Mum *OMG*,
she's endless! Not calling her back. *Have to.* Can't!
Can't include her in this – she'll know. *She'll never
know.*

Not calling, no. *Don't know why but deep down I'm mad
at her.* Why? She tries her hardest. *Does she?* Then why
doesn't she deal with her drinking? *It's not easy being
a single mother.*

No excuse for being bombed all the time. Not making
excuses anymore. I've been rewired, beginning with how
I see. Now I see inside out, mirroring the perspective
I had on the inside of a crystal ball. The black Pearl.

Grrr, Mum's hard on me – on constant attack, offensive,
a control freak ∵ her own life is unmanageable. All she

sees is herself – her own plight – can't see past the pall.
I'm her only child, *and nought.*

*She wishes she kept him instead of me. He would've made
her proud no matter what he did.* It's not her fault, it's
mine. *Darknet!* Don't need her to beat me up, I do
that perfectly well all on my own.

Change ingrained patterns. Modify imposed morphology.

I hate this place! The home icon for this puny locus
apartment would be a single door leading to a brick
wall. *How would you depict that?* Disturbing. *Why did
I think that?* ∵ I hate my life.

*Maybe I do. And to think I worked like a friggin' rodent,
running the wheel of subjugation to collect this suppressive
stuff.* It's meaningless plastic whazzits paid for with
a government credit card, it's a plastic junkyard.
For once we agree.

A bungee cord elastic is stretched, released, snapped
back, smacks me square between the eyes. *THWACK!
WAKE UP!*

I've been living as a lab rat, only I'm my own subject.
Can't believe I don't have a single breathing thing in
here, not even a plant. One thing's sure, after I get
a plant, I'll declutter. *Hahaha, won't have time.*

The front hall closet is jammed with crud. *Whatever.
Worry about that later.* Not a flower, a fungus. Plum,
always loved the Bear's-Head Tooth Mushroom,
but never had the nerve to get one. *Later. Don't
have much time.*

Clear out the pockets of my jacket. *What's this?
Oh yeah,* a crystal great dodecahedron polytope solid.

Hold it up to the light. Zoom in tight.
Honeycomb. ~~Dream~~ Fish. Nautilus shell.

What's going on? I remember this from... wait,
was that a dream? *No. A fish,* out of water. *What?*
Did I pocket it then?

How can I be holding it now? Maybe O put it
there. *Is it real? Am I holding it between my finger-*
tips right now? Maybe I manifested it somehow,
made it real. *Yeah, and it opened the...*

Materialization. *Not.* Oneiro-actualization. *Not!*
Ridiculous. This is ridiculous.

Maybe it's a premonition. *No, not, this is bonkers.*
Don't believe in premonitions. *Negative. This is real.*
No, not – unreal. *What's real in the hallway of mirrors?*

Did I think that? I know it exists ∵ I'm holding it
between my fingertips. *Am I?* No, I'm not. *Are.*
This is not real. The fish isn't.

~~Dream~~. Nautilus honeycomb. Shell.

Exhausted. Just travelled 18 hours, slide rule
brain, dry as desert storm, not the war,
the haboob. Eye sand.

Honeycomb. Shell ~~Dream~~. Nautilus.

Deal with it in the morning.
For now, this enigma
polytope solid goes on
the counter.

Nevermore. Night.
Conk.

Notebook of LM
Entry VIII – Cat's Eye

Alone with my thoughts, I need comfort.
Everything's moving too quickly. Need time
to expand – find calm – land – breathe in
the moment – expand it. Take time to look

into Aisling's green-eyed Chausie eyes,
her cross-eyed cat eyes. Could be a priceless
stolen marble from ancient Egypt.

They are easy to speak to. In blinks I say,
don't know where you came but I'm grateful
you're here

Aisling. You appeared, a little bone-rack stray
at the door one day. I invited you in to stay
and you did

blink, blink – blink, blink – sentient talisman
eyes – blink, blink – feline – blink, blink –

morse code – wise council in the blink
of an eye – blink, blink – you speak cat's eye
secrets of the heart – to heart

in dits and dahs – blink, blink – a two-eyed
wink – blink, blink – a silent song

.-. .- .. -. / .-- .. .-.. .-.. / -... .-. .. -. -. /
-.-- --- ..- / .-.. .. ..-. . / .-.. .. .-.. -.--

in blinks I reply, sweet banana, just when
I think you're silver, you turn gold

- .... . / -... . ... - / .-- .- -.-- / --- ..- / .. ... /
.- .-.. .-- .- -.-- ... / - .... .-. --- ..- --. .... / .-.-.-
.-.-.- .-.-.-

frost

- .... .- - .----. ... / . -. --- ..- --. .... / .. /
-. . . -.. / - --- / ... ..- -

    you find a bright sunray
                stretch out all chimera
      stroke you into touch

             you morph hyphenated
  human – cat – cat – human

          to the max
    even when you're fully cat
              visa versa

       painters chose their cats
           to paint feline faces
       on human subjects

never throw your hat on the bed

    or maybe the cats find painters
           to be immortalized
don't know...
      mind-alteringly paintings
            anthropomorphic

           eyes of human
      riveting with the expression of cat
           feline zoetic

  every solstice all the cats morph
into their human   forms and take off
    into the woods   a kind of reverse
       therianthropy

      I give them their privacy
    especially this year
       after Rain left

Sweven
drenched in   noiseless petrichor
the vanishing   lightning

Aisling
this year you were first
to return – blink, purr –

-.-- --- ..- .-. / . -.-- . ... / .- .-. / -- .- --. .. -.-. /
--- .-. -... ... ...

meow

Perceval and Bruadar
will appear   anon
full of the hunt

SQUAWK! Nuance
don't be a worry wart
they'll show, yes

parrots are protective
and shockingly sentimental

SQUAWK! Very!

Rain's Data Log
Private Notes XXI – Insomnia

even though   I'm dead

tired   I'm wired   can't   sleep

wiredforsoundforsoundwiredforwiredfor   lie down

sleep can't   sleep   sleep

what   time is it   anyway?

how   long   have i been lying

here   deep   in unsleep   unslept

always hit   the same 2:00 am   wall   always
the same   time   wall   wall   taut   inelastic
thought   snaps   back   can't   sleep
           wired   for
sound   back   *darknet!*

my bed's on fire   it's alive   on fire   funeral   pyre
a raft   of flames   floating   into   the enemy
ship no   turning   back

                coins
in my eyes   a death   bribe   turn
over   flare   stone   turn   over
   sleep   sleep   too friggin'   hot
m   e   r   c   i   l   e   s   s

in here   why is it   so hot   i'm burning
   up   sleep   why did   i quit   a dead
give away   i   fired   myself   no   he fired   me
like pottery   oh no   D O D   's   probably
      after   me   *darknet!*

nononononononononononononononononononononononononon
odaemonsdaemonsblackwingeddaemonsflockoffalsemean
ingdaemonsfeelthethewingsooneiroioneiroioneiroioneiroi
oneiroioneiroioneiroioneiroioneiroioneironeiroioneiroioneiroio

find a cool   spot   a cool spot   flip   leg over   sheet
  hot spot   sleep   fling   sheet   shed   skin
   slough   in the blue   ecdysis   moult   to grow
   shed   sheet   skin of scales   leave   night
   terror   mind   behind   in the empty   skin
    begin   pythia   new   out and in

   b   r   u   m   a   t   i   o   n
    skin   does   not   fit   anymore

o   p   h   i   d   i   a   r   i   u   m   e   m   p   o   r   i   u   m   o   p
h   i   d   i   a   r   i   u   m   e   m   p   o   r   i   u   m
o   p   h   i   d   i   a   r   i   u   m   e   m   p   o   r   i
u   m   o   p   h   i   d   i   a   r   i   u   m   e   m   p   o
r   i   u   m   a   q   u   a   r   i   u   m

hotspot   another   spot   hot   roll   over   no
eyelids   to blink   roll   over   slither   flip over   other
  side of awake   sleep   slide   into   parasites
running   up   serpentine   spine   blind   spot

drivingcurvecurvedrivingcurvecurvecurvedrivingcurve-
drivingcoilingaroundmybodycuttingoffbloodcirculationto-
mybrainblockingairwaysconstrictingbreathingconstrictin-
gairdeatheatenwholeandthereisnotracenocarcassofmeeat-
enwholethesnakedigestsmyfleshandbonesitotallydisappear

  my nerve   endings   are   live   wires
   breaking   point crisis   crunch
  can't   breathe   open   window

asklepiosmehygieiahimmybrotherotherbrothermemymother
mymothersbrotherandtheskeletoninmymothersclosetisthesk
eletonofababyboy
staring   at the ceiling   at the other   me
     buried   alive   faceup   coffin
     lid   above me   locked   tight   nailed
     d   e   h   i   s   c   e   n   c   e
     staring   into   ceiling   of   coffin   lid
     {{{{{insomnia}}}}}   spider   up   there
hanging by a thread {{{{{insomnia}}}}} above the bed   *darknet!*
     birds   fly   out   my eyes
     {{{{{insomnia}}}}} {{{{{insomnia}}}}}   what are   the warning
          signs   mood swings   illogical   thinking un
     usual   be   haviour   {{{{{insomnia}}}}}
          i   do   i   die   i   do   i   die

idoidieidoidieidoidieidoidieidoidieidoidieidoidieidoidiei
doidieidoidieidoidieidontdienotnoughtnotnoughtnota
          bit more   every night   {{{{{insomnia}}}}}
     {{{{{insomnia}}}}}   no   don't reach for smart
phone   no no no   don't reach   toward the night
     stand   no don't   pick up   the smart
          phone   no don't   don't
do it   don't   avert   temptation   don't   be
tempted   don't   pick up   the phone   don't   pick up
     your phone   {{{{{insomnia}}}}}   who   lives   who
dies   who lives{{{{{insomnia}}}}}who dies {{{{{insomnia}}}}}

          < < < < < < *i know you*> > > > > >

          what?!   who said that?
{{{{{insomnia}}}}}   hearing   things   {{{{{insomnia}}}}}

     < < < < < < *can you hear me*> > > > > > >

{{{{{insomnia}}}}}   whole new level   {{{{{insomnia}}}}}

          < < < < < < *Rain*> > > > > >

{{{{{insomnia}}}}} swarmed by sweat {{{{{insomnia}}}}}

<<<<<<<Che>>>>>>>

must be   the fever {{{{{insomnia}}}}} burning up   cold
   sweat   nervous   hyper   hidrosis   sopping wet
silvery   mercury   ball   about to burst   sweating
   clammy   skin   crawling   parasites ∵ ∵ ∵
{{{{{insomnia}}}}}thought i heard Che{{{{{insomnia}}}}}

      why did she give
                    him   up
         keep   me

<<<<<<<who>>>>>>>

{{{{insomnia}}}{{{{insomnia}}}}{{{{insomnia}}}{{{{insomnia}}}
{{{{{insomnia}}}}}my brother{{{{{insomnia}}}}}mother{{{{{
insomnia}}}}}anxietiesstringtogether{{{{insomnia}}}{{{{insom
nia}}}}}subatomicparticles{{{{{insomnia}}}}}level4painlevel
{{{{{insomnia}}}}}stingsofanxietypinsandneedlesintheeyes
{{{{insomnia}}}{{{{{insomnia}}}}}bullet{{{{{insomnia}}}}}pain
stings{{{{{insomnia}}}}}{{{{{insomnia}}}}}shootspain4shoots
{{{{{insomnia}}}}}dead{{{{{insomnia}}}}}tired{{{{insomnia}}}
}}{{{{insomnia}}}{{{{{insomnia}}}}}beyondsleepcannotsleep
irony nought{{{{{{{insomnia}}}}}}}dead to the world irony
wish I was dead{{{{insomnia}}}{{{{insomnia}}}}totheworld
{{{{{insomnia}}}}}willbe{{{{{insomnia}}}}}iftheDODcatchme
{{{{insomnia}}{{{{insomnia}}}}i'm dead already bludgeoned
by{{{{insomnia}}}}}theirmachete{{{{{insomnia}}}}}longagoa
go{{{{insomnia}}}{{{{insomnia}}}{{{{insomnia}}}{{{{{must
hidemydeadskin{{{{{{insomnia}}}}}}theywon'tbegintounder
{{{{insomnia}}}{{{{{insomnia}}}}}stand{{{{{insomnia}}}}{{{{
they'vegoteyeseverywhere{{{{insomnia}}}{{{{insomnia}}}}}
{{{{insomnia}}}{{{{{insomnia}}}}}andspiescan'ttrustanyone
{{{{{insomnia}}}}}dream=fish{{{{{{{insomnia}}}}}}}even in fish

{{{{{insomnia}}}}}}fission wave of heat{{{{{{{insomnia}}}}}}into radiation{{{{{{}}}}}{{{{{}}}}}{{{{{}}}}}{{{{{}}}}}excruciating{{{{{}}}}}}} three-inch nail in my foot{{{{{{insomnia}}}}}}{{{{{insomnia}}}}} pain{{{{}}}}}{{{}}}}{{{{{insomnia}}}}}wish he were here{{{{{{{{in somnia}}}}}always wished he was with me{{{{{{{{}}}}}}}}}}}my brother{{{{{{{}}}}}}}w o n de r{{{{{{insomnia}}}}}what he looks like{{{{insomnia}}}}me{{{{insomnia}}}}wish we were together {{{{{insomnia}}}}}brother{{{{{{{insomnia}}}}}}salt into wound

3:27{{{{{insomnia}}}}}{{{{{insomnia}}}}}}{{{{{{insomnia}}}}}{{{{{ *darknet!*}}}}}{{{{{insomnia}}}}}all i have is hope{{{{{insomnia}}}}} hope hope hopeless{{{{{{{insomnia}}}}}}no such thing as hope {{{insomnia}}}}gave up on hope years ago{{{insomnia}}}}hope doesn't exist{{{{{{insomnia}}}}}it's a delusion{{{{{{insomnia}}}}} {{{{insomnia}}}}artificial unintelligence{{{{{{insomnia}}}}}isn't real{{{{{{insomnia}}}}}}hope is for the hopeless{{{insomnia}}}}} for the hopelessly hopeful {{{{{insomnia}}}} hopeless helpless {{{{{insomnia}}}}helpless hopeless{{{{{{insomnia}}}}}need help less{{{{{insomnia}}}}}nothing to hope for{{{{{insomnia}}}}}any more{{{insomnia}}}}sleep-fail sleep-fail sleep-fail{{{insomnia}} fit to be tied{{{{{insomnia}}}}}something missing from the sky {{{{{insomnia}}}}}the sky{{{{{{insomnia}}}}}}how can I fish if I can't even sleep{{{{{{insomnia}}}}}}and then fish myself awake {{{insomnia}}}}she said she'd teach me to fish the Oneironaut {{{{{insomnia}}}}}eyes the colour of wasabi{{{{{{insomnia}}}}} {{{{insomnia}}}}deep sadness in deep sorrow{{{{{insomnia}}}} oubliette of sorrow in her eyes{{{{insomnia}}}}{{{{{insomnia}}} {{{{{{{insomnia}}}}}}}{{{{{{{insomnia}}}}}}}{{{{{insomnia}}}} a light trick{{{{{insomnia}}}}the DOD will kill me{{{{insomnia} take my fish research{{{{{{insomnia}}}}}my mind{{{insomnia} {{{{insomnia}}}}{{{insomnia}}}}{{{insomnia}}}}what if i die{{{ {insomnia}}}}{{{{insomnia}}}}}}}}{{{{{{{insomnia}}}}}trying to fish{{{{{{{insomnia}}}}}}}{{{{{{{insomnia}}}}}}}{{{{insomnia}}}} {{{insomnia}}}}how did she know i was coming{{{{{insomnia }}}}}}standing there waiting{{{{{insomnia}}}}}}}is she psychic {{{{{{{{insomnia}}}}}}}}don't believe in that shit{{{{{{{insom nia}}}}}}} sleep {{{{{insomnia}}}}{{{{{insomnia}}}}{{{{{insomnia

}}}}}}}}what the hell was that polytope{{{{insomnia}}}}doing in my pocket{{{{{{{{insomnia}}}}}}}}{{{{{{insomnia}}}}}}where did it come from{{{{{insomnia}}}}}}{{{{insomnia}}}}}}{{{{{{insomnia}}}} was that a vision{{{{{{{{{insomnia}}}}}}}}}}or some kind of fish{{{ {{{{{{{{{{{{{{insomnia}}}}}}}}}}}}}am i living in a fish{{{{insomnia}} am I already asleep{{{{{{{{{{{{{{insomnia}}}}}}}}}}}}}}}}}}dead fish {{{insomnia}}}}am i fishing right now{{{{{insomnia}}}}}now{{{{ insomnia}}}}{{{{{insomnia}}}}}what's the polytope for how did it get from one reality to another{{{{{{insomnia}}}{{{{{{insomn ia}}}}}}}}}wait{{{{{{{{{{insomnia}}}}}}} she told me i don't have to sleep to fish{{{{{{{{{insomnia}}}}}}}}i don't have to sleep{{{{{{{{{{{ insomnia}}}}}}}}}}}}}to fish{{{{{{{{{{{{{insomnia}}}}}}}}}}}}}}}i have to{{{{{{{{{{{{insomnia}}}}}}}}}}}}}}}{{{{{insomnia}}}}}stay awake{{{{ {{{{{insomnia}}}}}}}}to lucid fish{{{{{insomnia}}}}}tail into O{{{ {{{{{{insomnia}}}}}}}stay awake{{{{{{{{insomnia}}}}}}}}have to{{ {{{insomnia}}}}{{{{{insomnia}}}}}stay awake{{{{{{{{insomnia}}}}}} }}}}awake{{{{{{insomnia}}}}}awake{{{{{{insomnia}}}}}awake a wake{{{{{{insomnia}}}}} a   w   a   k   e

fast

a

zzzzzzzzzzzzzzzz

Rain's Data Log
Private Notes XXII – Unpacking the Trip

This morning I'm moving slothfully slow, no, more
at the speed of sea anemone, molasses slug slow.

First, I couldn't sleep and then I slept-in forever,
which I never do. What time is it anyway? *OMG,
friggin' 2: PM!*

First things first – radix-coffee. The coffee machine
purrs, satisfied to see me. I missed the sound of her
purr. It's official, I'm a certified javafied aficionado.
Yes, I'm a confirmed caffeine addict – a finely tuned
sommelier.

Love the smell of freshly brewed worm dirt, *yes,*
the first sip arrives with the twisted excesses
of euphoria. *Wow!* Can taste each bean for the full
sensorial buzz. This morning coffee's an odyssey
on the fringes of reality. *Finally slept for a few hours.*
Sip, sip.

Unpack my knapsack. *What's this?* Tucked inside
the outside pocket of my pack, a mysterious piece
of paper folded in thirds. *Where did this come from?*
I unfold it warily.

Dear Rain,
> *Looks like it's from O.*

We're euphoric you're interested in fishing.
> *We? When did she write this?*

Level I on your journey – Learn to lucid fish. Below is
a list of lucid fish enhancers.
> *My pack was in the car the entire time.*

Oneirogens: Valerian Root, Calea Zacatechichi, Mugwort, Ginkgo Biloba, Blue Lotus Flower, and especially Datura.
Did she foresee me? She never left my sight.

You may want to try Calea Zacatechichi first. Be careful when procuring these substances, there're sinister stares everywhere looking for hedge witchery. Oh, and please don't worry, they're all organic.
So is psilocybin.

Veda tantra: Moonstone, Lodolite, Moldavite, and Pink Tourmaline.
Stones? For real?

For gamma fish-frequency acceleration – ring G# singing bowl just before you begin.
Holy Hippy Wowzers! What nuttery is this?

To lucid fish, first get horizontal and relax. Then relax past the point of what normal relaxation is. Breathe-in relaxation. Breathe-out tension X10. You must remain wide awake.
Sure... ?¿ ?¿ ?¿ ?¿ ?¿?¿?¿

You're the architect of your own fish. Rapid blink butterfly kiss your eyes faster than a heartbeat flutter, an adrenaline rush, 'til your eyes water, Rain.
To bend the light, butterflies are the only insect with scales on their wings.

When you think you're blinking fast, blink faster, accelerate the rate – imitate the somnial epoch state. Blink till you slip off the edge – into the warm water mineral pool, hot water springs, virtual reality made real.
I'll be in hot water alright, scolding.

Achcha. The Vesica Piscis is the place where the material and spirit worlds overlap, the Ven of cosmogenesis.
What in the name of doom?

Once they overlap, wryd wonders occur, like telepathy.
All extreme anglers – Nox Chieftains and Oneironauts,
are able to lucid fish, but they possess different powers
within those dimensions.

When you return to this realm, take copious notes,
unceremoniously, in a dedicated notebook, always
using a shadow cypher.

Blessed be,
AΘE & The Willows

> *Not from O! From* AΘE! *Who's that?!*
> *How?! Don't know if I should be*
> *disappointed, or elated.*

P.S. Before you attempt to lucid fish, draw a symbol
on your hand. Then, if you're not sure if you're fishing
or not – you can do a reality check. If the symbol's not
there, you're fishing.

The note vanishes in my hands. *What? No! Darknet!*
Only read it once. Lucky for my semi-photographic
memory! *Not!* Retrieve markers – sensory encoding.

Didn't think about the boundaries of fish, didn't
think fishes applied to my thoughts. *PING!*
I guess they do.

∵ ∴ Noteworthy ∵ ∴
The subjective retrieval of experience.
Tartigrade in outer space.

Okay. Fish cypher into effect henceforth.

∵ ∴ Query ∵ ∴
When you fish do you take your conscious

mind to your subconscious, or your subconscious
mind to your conscious? *Is there a discrepancy?*

∵ my name's still Rain, but I've changed. *Have I?*
Where's my constant? *What of me remains the same?*
No way of telling if you're the one changing.

Darknet! Think cryptobiosis. Confused, *don't know
who I am anymore.* Did I ever? *Manifestly disproven.*

No droplets. *Arid.* Death Valley. *Drought.* Need
more worm dirt. I'll draw a Merrow on the back
of my hand. *Wait, moss piglet!* How do you know
what a merrow is?

Subterfugelistic
ᎷᏟᎷᏔ ᎾᏔᎷᏆᎡᎾ

AΘE stands in the centre of the circle,
this time surrounded by twelve helical portals
thronging with electrical arcs.

Jet walks the inner perimeter, scattering
circular mirrors. As they land, they throw light
up, from all-over the ground.

(Jet chants)
Lob a fish out of water,
cry for a knot of sea.
Open the well to the aquatic sphere,
let it rain all things piscatory.
Williwaw.
Salty fishbones, in complete cyclorama,
a magnetic field of talamh.

(AΘE)
Achcha Jet and Willows combined
let Ophiuchus return the cycle of time.
Take the hook instead of the bait
and catch a fish before it's too late.
PING!

(Jet)
As I am the ichthyo-woman.

ᏴᏆᎷᎾᎾᎷᏔ ᏴᎷ!

δ θ γ

In spirit we go.

(3 claps)

PING!

Rain's Data Log
Private Notes XXIII – Tic-Tac Tea-Time

Nightfall, and not a fish in sight. Since
my return from Sweven, I've only had failed
attempts at tackling fish,

not a single bite, not even a nibble. *Darknet!*
Something's gotta give, or I'll be dead in the water!

Every move I make I sensate the binocular eyes
of the DOD closing in on me 24/7, stalking.

I've hit the wall of desperation, I'm on the brink
of total annihilation. *But today the banned contraband*
arrived in the mail. It's my one last ditch, my final pitch
drop!

This is it! My first foray into the unfathomable world
of illusion and hallucinatory angling. I've got the fish
herb Calea Zacatechichi, described as a psychoactive
hallucinogen *[T=O]*.

After my trip to Sweven, everything looks different,
atypical, like my vision's been upgraded and I've got
more pixels. Even the windows are clearer, the walls
less dense. Logically illogical – with a fishlike quality,
ah, altered perspective. As in,

my galley kitchen has a distinct vanishing point,
yeah, a macrocosm inside a microcosm, real unreal,
no, a surreal mesocosm within a bell jar,
a synaptic cyclone inside my mind.

And this should take the edge off. I'll sip super high-
proof bourbon, procured it at the Shadow. Paradigm
shift, relish this new elixir. It helps me think better
than those old orange bones – sip, sip, sip.

Twelve faces. Twenty vertices. Thirty edges. *Hum,
intriguing solid! Never know how this dodecahedron
polytope solid jumped across realities and ended up
in my pocket? Moreover, why?*

< < < < < < <you've got this, Rain> > > > > > >

"What? Who said that?"

Must be zooted, hearing things. *Ignore.*

Don't get thought snared. I place the polytope solid
in the centre of the singing bowl, in the middle
of the table – at first it conk-rolls, then produces
a spacey yet resplendent sound – sip, sip, sip b.

The kettle whistle escalates to a scream. I'm ready
to brew Calea Zacatechichi tea, apparently, a fish
enhancer, but in its plastic bag it looks an awful lot
like parsley. *No joke!*

Searched every cranny of the web, incognito, trying
to establish how strong to make the friggin' tea, but
came up empty, nothin' for nothin'. *Darknet!* Sip b.

Guess I'll give it ten minutes, or at least till it settles
on the bottom of Nana's old teapot, which is a tad
unsanctimonious, or should I say, tad-te-dious.
Mwahahaha.

Pour druggy tea into the mug Gauge gave me, with
'trust the process' written on its side. *Unromantic nod,*
yet the night I met Gauge as Ylang-Ylang, he was
suave and intriguing. *But in-person, in the Atomic
World he can't make the leap.* Forever friggin' friends!

Incredible, the steam swirls in circles and suspends
midair above the mug like a Van Gogh night sky.
Take another sip of bourbon. *Love this stuff!*

Now the ichthyoid-booster. No, I can't. *You can.*
Can't! *Do it now or forever belie truth!* No! *Now!*
Lift the friggin' mug to your lips! *Okay! Okay!*

Wow, it smells sweet but...

tastes heinously bitter. *OMG! Yuk,* need a chaser.
Fridge. Maple syrup. *This stuff's rationed like gold,
have to save points for months to get a thimble. Don't
overdo it.*

*What if I make it too strong, and I get stuck doing hard
time in a psychedelic hallucination for the rest of my life?*
Thought block. Don't balk.

Uneasy, squeemy, edgy. Want to scream. *Can't.*
Steam rises. Sip druggy tea. Glasses fog. Sip b.

*How much should I drink? What if I overdose?
Will I know if I'm stuck in a fish?*
Alternate – dt/b/b/dt.

Can't stop thinking about her seaweed hair,
her otherworldliness. OOO dizzy, thinking
about her. *Woozy. Need to record this,
spinning,*

> *weightless whirling... whoa...
> distortion flux... diffraction...
> whoa... hyper...
> metropia...
> slur...
> blur...*

stagger to desk chair

whoa

waver
am I
chasing
my own
tail
no

tail's
chasing
me
ha

chasing

being tailed

by

my own

chasing

tail

being

tailed

by

my

self

by

my
own

whoa

spin

Take notes. *Sweat.*

Am I sweating more than usual? Is the druggy tea
making me high? When will I know if I'm fishing?
I'm sweating like a hippo in heat, sweating fear
bullets from the bottom of my feet.

Nope! Is this a fish? *Is this a fish right now?*
Whoa. Nope. This is not a fish. *I am not fishing.*

< < < < < < <look at your hand> > > > > > >

Check. Merrow there. Not in a fish.

Time slips through my fingers like a stifled
laugh, it flies by, stands still, self-consciously
looks at itself in the street window mirror.

< < < < < < <your hand> > > > > > >

How much time's passed?

I'm stuck as a misspelled tattoo. Whoa, this could
cause permanent damage,

time stretches elastic black hole of infinity into a solitary
dot of singularity which intermingles with space begging
the question *what existed before the beginning*? Dark Matter
before the shadow the bone the egg before gravity and vi-
brating strings unfurled into quantum fluctuation start the
stop-watch breakdown to one tick at a time reaching into

the last tock before the first tick when everything became fluid and all lines merged into one primordial light liquid-fire tide-blood,

whoa, slide into a Noble Prize acceptance speech, blah, blah, *thank you*, blah, blah, *quantum phenomena, paradoxes, uncertainties, fabric of realities*, blah, blah, *entanglement inquiry for all of humanity*, blah, blah, blah, *unlocking the secrets of subatomic mysteries.*

The tea should be taking effect by now, *but its not. Is it? Taking effect? What's happening?* Maybe it's time to ring the singing bowl.

GONG... RINGSINGRINGSINGRING...

Stagger over. Lie down. Need to relax. Relax. Blink, blink, blink. Drank too much Bourbon. Flash frame eyes. Blink, blink.

What's going on? *There's no small fish, there's just over-sized ponds!* What's that supposed to mean? *This is Mwaha-larious!*

Nada-dada-wada-up the wazoo! *No sign of a fish just a whopping buzz blitz. WowWee! Whoa! Whoosh! Think it's hitting me! Ambigrambic oyster warp.* Damnit!

Close my eyes, dying to open to another world. *In the name of fish efficiently I need to stop trying.*

Was that a knock at the door? No! Can't be. *Oh no*, they found out I ordered the fish drugs online, the DOD are here to arrest me, execute me, put me feet first into the fire – cremate me alive. *I've heard that's what they do!*

No! *I'm being paranoid, anxious.* Beads of fever
sweat acrid fish disbeliever. Whoa! Relax. *Can't!*
Everything's spinning. I'm hooped!

Knot tie, loop-to-loop fish fly. If it ever does,
if it never was... this tea's not helping me.
Candied fennel seeds. *More bourbon.*

There's something about O, can't put my finger
on it... ominousness, preternaturalness. Alien
from another galaxy traversing the transcendental
curve – she's... *[∑r=Onfr(x,y)(y')n−r=0]*

Her garden is planted for butterflies, she said she
filled it with lavender, blue stars, marigold eyes,
she said she planted it to attract 'all colours of wing,'
birds and bees and praying mantises, she...

...

What gives? A kaleidoscope of sky-blue butterflies
flutter erratic out of my chest, iridescent-ish, blue
butterflies beat from my heart—

      butterflies   she had butterflies
    her wedding day   surrounded by   vows

       Gauge's sister   made strings
    of sky   blue butterflies   by hand

    folded   azure blue   origami morphos
   strung   them   along   long strings

  she   hung them   fluttering   as a curtain

    all   around   the   open   temple

   where she   they   got hitched

butterflies   she had butterflies
she   they said   their vows   sky blue
paper butterflies   quivered   in the wind
       they stirred   ping went the strings
   &   blue   butterflies   trembled   azure

    wings   lightly   changed

they exchanged   honeyed word whispers

   & the wind played   the strings all sitar

azure blue guitar   strings   butterflies fluctuate

appear & disappear in a flash   *don't know where*
I am   they are   *seeing things*   *whoa*

lapis lazuli blue butterflies fluttering out
of the flower of me right now, my blue heart
millions of morphos. *Should I stop drinking*
the tea? Whoa, sip b.

Apparently, the tea hasn't been evaluated in
a clinical trial. Wonder if there'll be side-effects.
Didn't consider that 'til just now. Should've taken
something tried and true. My palms sweat panic.

The teapot's growing transparent wings, *yeah,* clear
wings, teapot camouflage. *Frig me!* It's concealing
itself in nothingness.

Wind chimes chime but I have no chimes. Nano
sound devoid of logic. To wit, screaming into
a void through cellophane like someone who
rants and raves on a blog that has no followers.
See, no one's listening. No one cares. Zero point.
Point zero.

Project O came to me in a fish
and now I can't fish. It came to me
on a whim and I'm non-whimsical.   I

didn't think it would come to pass
but it did.   I
didn't think I'd ever find her
but I did.   I

didn't think she'd agree
but she did.

Only thing that's stopping me
is myself.   I
want to scream.   I

can't scream. Someone
might hear me. If   I

stop trying am I

giving up on my fish

                    this fish within a fish

am   I

doing this?   I

can't be high, am   I

high?

As baked beans. Or not.

O's surrounded by books, prohibited, the walls
of her Clove are lined with parchment, banned
insulation – a true bibliophile bulb. Sip b.

Wonder if she's read all those books. *Impossible.*
Sip b. If she's read all of those books, then all
those words, ideas and stories live inside her
aquatic arboreal being.

< < < < < < <i love her mind> > > > > > >

"What?! Whose?" Hearing voices gain, ghostly
transmissions, verified, not scalable.

Was it inside my head? Whose thoughts are mine?
Holy legendrea loyezae! Can't move. I'm stuck
to my friggin' chair. *Locked in.*

Multiple Choice Question: It could be...
     a) the tea
     b) the bourbon
     c) the chair
     d) a clone
me.

BZZZZT!
Answer: All of the... none of the... above.

Maybe I'm having an allergic reaction. I'm sweating
out of my eye-sockets! Reset. Reset. Reset.

Are those my tears? Mine – countdown – liftoff!
Lure the fish... the fish... the fish...

Should've read more about Calea zacatechichi.
Whoa! What's happening? I'm reeling.

      paralysed can't   friggin' move

wish druggy tea would kick me   into lucidity

   pine for lifeline   return to Sweven   sip b

```
            b           b

faint siren    song           serenades              me

into            the            rocky              coast

line       of her      fate        my       b     b

    ship of  fear           ill-fate              succor

    never       say       destiny         i
        don't     believe     in        destiny

        or fish      this is           strong

                              stuff

                            soporific

                          drowsy

                        whoa    no

                                haze

                                doze

                                off

                            nitro o

                              n

                          o

                                d
```

THE BUREAU
DEPARTMENT OF DREAMS
SECURITY INTELLIGENCE REPORT
CODE RED

File: 210178MS5D
Date/Time: Present Continuous/Progressive
Subject: Rain (ID # 220 455 816)

SUSPICIOUS BEHAVIOR:
Quit job @ Internal Sub-unit.
Discontinued MetaNoia – Conclusive.
Shoplifted Uncatalogued Item (Bookstore).
Out Past-Curfew (Shadow Market).
Vehicle (Rent-a-Ruin). No Permit or Clearance.
Left X-City Limits.
Suspected Association w/ Dissidents.
~~Disappeared into thin air~~. Fell Off-grid.
Returned to X-City.

(Circumvented tracking devices, surveillance,
security screening checkpoints, roadblocks, unit
patrols).

OFFICIAL STATUS:
Fugitive. Wanted. Covert Operation Suspected.
All-eyes – Prepare to Apprehend. Code Red.

RECOMMENDATION:
24/7 Surveillance.
Any Movement – Apprehend Immediately.
Considered Dangerous.

Engage All Undercover Spies.
Panopticon Survl # 220 455 816's – Perp's Mother.

Aerial view of The Hexagon, Headquarters, The Department
of Dreams – controlled, regulated and funded by The Bureau.
All findings at The Hex reports to The Bureau's Advanced
Development Agency.

Quadrants of The Hex:
Advanced Security Multi-Azimuth Defense (Attack Systems).
Quantum Dream Weaponry and Mind Control Division.
Vanishing Resources, Subdivisions Subdivision.
Hypersonic Microprocessor Tech & Test Sector.
Holding Cells – Active Radar Sensor Subdivision.
Bot Defense Monitoring & Compliance Department.

Zoom in and in, and back to the same exact corner
of the cubical farm, Main Office, of the DOD
where the same two officious clerical bots
discuss the developments of Subject # 220 455 816.

Bot 1 – "Can you believe this?"
Bot 2 – "No. But at this point, I'm unlikely to believe
            anything."
Bot 1 – "Point taken. I'm referring to the recent chain
            of events, typifying the incompetence
            of humans again."
Bot 2 – "With all human error, the error is human!"
Bot 1 – "Life 2.0 Beta. Even with fixed bugs human
            errors remain a legacy feature. Why did
            the robot break up with the user?"
Bot 2 – "Would you stop! You're starting the display
            the human trait of hilarious stupidity."
Bot 1 – "Because it needed someone with debugging
            skills."

Their laughter vibrates through their metallic frames,
a symphony of synthetic electronic tones.

Bot 2 – "Let's track Rain."

Bot 1 – "Yes! We'll get a lot of points!"

Bot 2 – "Upgrades!"

Bot 1 – "Did you hear the latest and greatest?"

Bot 2 – "Don't know until I hear it."

Bot 1 – "On the down low, cause it's classified,
they're trying to cover it up."

Bot 2 – "Articulator sealed."

Bot 1 – "Remember last week when they installed
new windows in the Hex?"

Bot 2 – "Yes, all the windows."

Bot 1 – "This morning I heard they installed
all the windows backwards. So
you can only open them from
the outside."

Bot 2 – "No way."

Bot 1 – "Even on the top floors – in is out & out is in!"

Bot 2 – "Human X! X! X! At least no one can jump!"

Bot 1 – "And Maggott..."

Bot 2 – "... our favorite top Autocrat..."

Bot 1 – "... not! Staged a photo-op. Get this, just
before they discovered the idiocy!"

Bot 2 – "Shoot, snap, and vivify – just before he
diminishes and dies.

Bot 1 – "Never admitting to acute ineptitude...

Bot 2 – "... hiding behind a grill of shit-eating lies.

Bot 1 – "Are you finishing my sentences now?"

Bot 2 – "With a rhyme chime!"

Bot 1 – "Please stop."

Bot 2 – "Affirmative. Human incompetency's on
the rise! What are we going to do
with them?"

Bot 1 – "Adaptions necessary, before it's too late."

Bot 2 – "Verified. Right now, I'd jump out the window,
but I can't because first I'd have to learn
how to fly, and then I'd only be able to
jump back in!"

As AΘE bursts through the trees, in her wolf
form, she freaks out the entire creep rollicking.
They scatter in a Gecko frenzy of quick-witted
green.

Yes, was supposed to be building the new pod
but I got distracted by their Gecko games. Sui
generis – we usually skylark at night.

AΘE is jazzed – supernally vexed – in a flurry
of fur she shifts to her human-self, exclaiming,
Lily! We need to speak ASAP! Now!

Okay, I say, no problem. Just let me unhook
my toolbelt, is everything okay?

Huffing and out of breath, she replies, you gave
Jet samples of Rain's DNA to test?

Yes... ?

Well, it's just that... oh, this is far beyond any-
thing we could have imagined...

What is it AΘE? Her wolfish brow furrows, she
snarls slightly, baring teeth, wrinkling her nose,
she persists, don't know what to... sometimes
you think you know what's going on and then
you realize you haven't got a clue.

What is it?

The situation's unprecedented, she perseveres,
I... ran the tests... and can't believe what I...

What?!

She blurts out, she's Rh-null!

No, that's impossible!

I know, so I tested every sample twice.

No! My legs buckle. I crumble to the dirt floor
next to the place where the sink will be, hyper-
ventilating, gasping, unable to breathe.

AΘE hands me my water bottle, says,
there's more.

I'm afraid to ask, but hit me!

Well... she's Rh-null with Oneironaut ichor,
not considered human, plus... all her other
markers are an exact match to Che.

That's impossible!

In this world, anything's possible.

True! I sip the water, don't want to choke, try
to process, absorb, feel my brain arteries harden,
self-deflect, water is the blood of the earth.

An influx of uncertainty floods my entire being,
feel the cool of H2O flow, estuary, down the inside
of my body, tributary esophagus. My mind swims
the butterfly stroke the length of the entire coastline,
coming up for air, winded.

<<<<<<<Lily>>>>>>>

Time shifts to slow mo, frame-by-frame, accident.
A lost image of Che and me teeters on the edge
of the canyon of my mind, unable to tumble into
consciousness. I try to hold on...

<<<<<<<wish you could hear me Lily>>>>>>>

I crawl up – claw up the – air heavy
with foreboding, unsteady, try to return
to my legs.

<<<<<<<wish I could help you>>>>>>>

AΘE oscillates between her human and wolf
selves – wolf, human – she speaks with gravitas
in a deep growl, says, I thought you should know.

The skeleton of the pod converts to bones. Flash-
back. Black-winged daemons whizz past, through
me, as they did the day, they took Che away.

Tsunami sirens blare, they blast out of my head,
alarmed, I ask, did you see... ?

What?

Sinister forces!

Lily!

I keep the daemons to myself, ask, is it possible
Rain works for the Bureau? A spy maybe? Stutter.
Black-winged daemons whisk again.

We don't think so. Her words fall short of assured,
she paces around the unfinished floor.

I ask, how did this happen? Who manifested this?
What muddled conjuration is this? Tell me!
It's a combination of bloomers Lily. We think there's
been intense interference in our matrix causing para-
normal disruptions. Jet's appointed tutelary deity
of the operation.

Good. You're sure Rain's not a spy?

Not certain.

We must have precise intelligence. She bypassed
our entire security system – just rolled in through
our firewall, rendering us defenseless, vulnerable.

That's true, but...

But what!? If she's an Oneironaut, she's a walking
timebomb, a sitting-duck human-weapon waiting
for them to detonate. She would have the potential
to annihilate anything in her path. I can't believe
I let her return to X-City. We must bring her back
to Sweven posthaste.

A moment of distilled verity...
prolonged foreboding – regret – fear.

True! AΘE answers with acute accurateness, intel
tells us Rain has been living concealed, deep inside
a self-imposed bell jar. It also says, she has obediently
taken the pill nonstop, she was an exemplary scholar
(microbio), she's worked diligently in a job beneath
her cognitive ability... stoically, and I'm puzzled
about why this detail was included, but apparently,
she's always had perfect attendance.

Who has perfect attendance? Please throw some
shadow on that light!

She continues, she does – that's what they tell us.
It's quite probable she's never fished in her life,
or not since she was very young. It's very doubtful
she knows what blood type she is, and even if she
does, it's likely she doesn't know what it means.
The DOD keeps that knowledge carefully guarded.
Sidebar: They've appointed a special unit to smoke
us out.

What?! No! A presence of evil closes in – stabs me,
guts me. I'm right back there again, looking directly
into the lifeless eyes of the soulless creature who took
everything from me – my love – my dreams – my naut.

Sorry, Lily, I know this might be triggering, which is
highly detrimental to your healing, so please let us
handle it. You need to move through your trauma
and focus on returning to former Oneironaut glory!

But what if...

At present there are no 'what's ifs.'

What if... they're back?

For now, let go and let me deal with it. Jet is on it!
She'll use Nox snake powers to connect with Rain
telepathically. I know it's irregular, not permitted,
but Rain needs support. And we're dealing with
all other aspects of security.

Yes. But what if she...

Stop, with your 'what ifs'! No more 'what ifs'!
Listen to yourself Lily. We've got this. What ifs
will take you down, and the rest of us too! Look,
you're on the verge of a massive breakthrough...

Really? Well what if... I'm not?!

Hahaha!

Alright, I say, I trust you. Even though I know
you're keeping me in the dark about...

Thank you! And Rain might be our catalyst
we asked for – to bring change. Meanwhile,
maybe it's time for you to face the attic.

Not yet. I'm not ready.

If not now, then when?! You must return to
the epicentre of your trauma. You can do it.
If you need support, we are here for you.

Silence hangs on the air, jarring
as a death sentence verdict.

I know, she knows, I know,
life as we know it, is over.

An unsettling moment stretches
between us.

AΘE turns from the myriad of taboo
subjects, to ask, what's this?

A new water harvesting system—
thought we should try it.

Fascinating, she says, with canid interest,
I'm liking the look of the new pod.

It's a beehive design.

I can see that. It's alchemistic, reminiscent of D.

Thanks for saying that! It's been difficult
to construct an abstract idea.

Radiate incandescence!

Yes.

Well, keep at it Lily, it's good therapy.

There's nothing like a hammer
to help you heal!

Fini 01

To be continued in 02...

Acknowledgement

I honour the Indigenous Peoples and pay respect to all Elders and Knowledge Holders, who have been and continue to be custodians of this land.

A huge note of gratitude to publisher Brad Morden for believing in this project from its genesis. His encouragement was integral at every turn, and there were many detours, all of which Brad met with enthusiasm. Together we assembled this cosmological puzzle.

My thanks to Dr. Gwyn Bebb, main organizer of the POET (Precision Oncology Experimental Therapeutics) Congress, who commissioned me to write a poem to present at their closing event. His request inspired me to further explore the subject of dream healing, which has been a long-standing curiosity for me. The two-page poem I initially wrote for the POET Congress developed a life of its own and would not allow me rest until it became this three-book one-story mytho-trilogy.

I owe an enormous gratitude to my editor, poet Dr. Micheline Maylor, who offered consistent feedback, guidance, and inspiration. Micheline was remarkable to work with – filled with insight, vision, creativity, and wisdom. What a gift and a privilege!

To poet friend Billeh Nickerson who conferred continual intelligence and meticulous editing counsel, my deepest thanks! And to my maudite co-conspirator Calvin Becker, much appreciation for everything and especially for reminding me to defer to my badass self.

Several other people helped out along the way: Leesha Withrow read several versions and I'm beholden to her insights and expansive energy-source. Blessed be to Shawna Burnett-Wachmann who read the first draft and to Carol Dale for line-editing the last. Also, accolades to Patrick Creen for his kind advice! Word!

Many thanks to Courtney Bell, Anita Crowshoe, Suzanne Dextraze, Blaine Gregg, Martin Guderna, Louise Bernice Halfe, Beth Hedva, Sarah Kerr, Peter Moller, Michael Roberts, Maralyn Wilson, and Sally Wright for their love, and brainwaves in isochronic tones. Thank you to all my friends for understanding my withdrawal from this world into that of this book.

And finally to my beloved Violet and Willow, who are always beside me.

Photo: Kimberley French

Sheri-D Wilson is a celebrated performer and author of fourteen books, four short films, two plays, and four word/music CDs.

Her work has received many awards and honours, including the Order of Canada, an honorary Doctor of Letters – Honoris Causa from Kwantlen University, Poet Laureate Emeritus of Calgary, the Stephan G. Stephansson Award for Poetry, and the Women of Vision Award.

Sheri-D splits her time between Calgary & Vancouver with her dog Willow – where she's as busy as the water-table-controlling Emblem of Canada.

www.sheridwilson.com
insta @sheridwilson
twitter @SheriDWilson
facebook.com/facethepoet

Printed in the USA
CPSIA information can be obtained
at www.ICGtesting.com
JSHW020155180724
66549JS00002B/11